Justice and Doubt

An Essay on the Fundamentals of Justice

By

Ilmar Tammelo, Sydney

Springer-Verlag Wien GmbH

1959

ISBN 978-3-662-38924-9 ISBN 978-3-662-39864-7 (eBook)
DOI 10.1007/978-3-662-39864-7

Contents

Dedicated to the memory of
Gustav Radbruch

Justice and Doubt

An Essay on the Fundamentals of Justice

By

Ilmar Tammelo*

Introductory

In the present essay I shall attempt to elaborate, by means of an analysis which relies heavily on contemporary philosophical thought, the notion of justice as it has come down to us in historical tradition. There are many excellent works on justice by classical as well as by modern writers, however, I do not know of any work in which contemporary philosophy has had sufficient opportunity to advance our understanding of this perennial concern of mankind. In view of the number of capital

---

* *Mag. iur* (Tartu, Estonia), *Dr. jur.* (Marburg, Germany), M. A. (Melbourne, Australia). Research Fellow, Department of Jurisprudence and International Law, University of Sydney, Australia; formerly *Privatdozent* in Jurisprudence and Legal Philosophy, University of Heidelberg.

For the initial stimulus of this essay my debt is to my lamented teacher Gustav Radbruch of Heidelberg. Heavy debts during its preparation were incurred to Professor Alexander Boyce Gibson of Melbourne for guidance on the early drafts, to Dr. Boris Bertelsons of Sydney for much challenging criticism, and to Professor Julius Stone for the influence of his treatise *The Province and Function of Law* (2nd ed. 1950) as well as for the benefit of constant interchange of ideas between us while the essay was taking its final form during my work with him at the Universities of Sydney and Harvard. My debts are great also to Professor Barna Horvath of the New School for Social Research in New York, to Professor Roderick M. Chisholm of Brown University in Providence, to Professor Samuel I. Shuman of Wayne University in Detroit, to Mr. Jaan Puhvel and Mr. K. Jaakko J. Hintikka of the Society of Fellows of Harvard University, to Dr. Stevan Glichitch of the University of Sydney, and to Miss Anita Pincas, B. A., of Sydney, who have read late drafts of the essay and offered valuable comments. For much assistance with the final form of linguistic expression I am indebted to Miss Zena Sachs, LL. B., of the University of Sydney and to my wife Hilda Tammelo.

I desire also to express my sincere appreciation to the Vice-Chancellor and the Research Committee of the University of Sydney for their assistance in making this work possible as part of the Research Programme of the Department of Jurisprudence and International Law of that University.

works on ethics, metaphysics, theory of knowledge, and logic published since the beginning of this century, we may be entitled to assume that fresh insights are to be found in them which would greatly benefit also inquiries into the fundamental principles of justice. Although I intend to avail myself of this source of information to a considerable degree, I do not believe that the modern is a self-value. I am aware that the evolution of thought occasionally takes regressive turns, so that in the learning of a given period much of value possessed by earlier generations may have become lost. Thus, in writing the present essay, I have not closed my mind to inspirations that the philosophical past, as far back as the pre-Sokratics, may provide for an inquiry into the fundamentals of justice. However, I feel that the fundamentals of any great human concern should be reconsidered in any new philosophical situation. New frames of basic reference should be given an opportunity to show what they could contribute to a fuller penetration into the problem.

Contemporary philosophy certainly contains more learning relevant for an inquiry into the fundamentals of justice than it has been in my power to canvass. Therefore I do not claim completeness for any part of my work, but would rather emphasise its limited scope and partial aims. But even as a sketch, I hope that it will prove of service in the quest for the principles of justice, if not by its merits then perhaps by its shortcomings. I hope that where my views do not meet with the reader's approval, they may awaken in him dissatisfaction and disquietude intense enough to stimulate his own thought towards more assured results.

While I am aware that the philosophical references in which I seek support for my inquiry can be but rather limited, I have nevertheless avoided confining myself within the walls of any particular philosophic school. Sensing a latent or potential unity among principal movements of contemporary philosophy, I have looked for guidance in various sources of fundamental thought, even though this has sometimes required going into radically antagonistic camps. In this search I have found that as antagonistic as the schools, for example, of logical positivism and of what is referred to as existentialism appear to be, they are in fact each preoccupied with different aspects of the subject matter of philosophy and so have produced insights which are often quite complementary. That philosophical schools are becoming more and more immune to each other's influences appears to be largely due to the fact that the ever increasing mass of philosophic learning permits only of an increasingly defective acquaintance of philosophers with each other's contributions. Contemporary philosophers must feel weary under the burden of philosophic learning accumulated over two thousand and five hundred years. No wonder that they feel impatient with each other and become incapable of an adequate scholarly communication! Seeking guidance in antagonistic schools of thought does, of course, carry the danger of falling into eclecticism. To avoid this danger, I have constantly striven to organise my thoughts into a sufficiently coherent system. I have not attempted, however, to build a closed and rigid system of the notions by means of which I have tried to apprehend the fundamental principles of justice. Such a system I feel would be worse than making certain concessions to eclecticism. Eclecticism, if not inordinate, has at least the merit of keeping thought moving in streams, however small and scattered, which may find a way to an ocean. It is one alternative to restricting thought within a pool in which philosophy must stagnate.

Since I have no total objection to any historical or contemporary philosophical system, I have not hesitated to employ terms which many would like to see banned from philosophy. Thus „Being", „Substance", „the Absolute", and „the *Summum Bonum*" occur in the following pages for purposes other than historical and critical exposition. This is because I feel that any penetration into a wide and intricate fundamental problem demands a considerable number of philosophical terms. Although I have created or adopted philosophical neologisms (for example, „precation", „sistence", „axiotic dignity"), employed hyphenation to indicate specific use of terms (*„ek-stasis", „con-ceptum"*, „hypo-thesis"), and given a specific sense to some terms in common use („surmising", „understanding", „care"), my resort to these devices, each of which has its drawbacks, has been very limited. I have dropped my inhibitions about the use of classical terms since I have hoped that those who would read the present essay would be able to dissociate their thoughts from the taint which may have become attached to these terms in doctrinal history. Most of the classical terms, for example, „ontology", „subsistence", „essence", are capable of acquiring new acceptable meanings in the new contexts in which they are used. Insofar as those terms remind us of the conquests of thought of which they have become symbols and carry warnings about aberrations into which the thought expressed by them has often entered, their value for us is twofold. They serve contemporary philosophic thought in providing it with a substantial part of its nomenclature. And they also keep alive our awareness of gratifying or frustrating past philosophical experiences, neither of which effects can be irrelevant for present and future philosophical work.

The inquiries which follow have been organised into six chapters placed between six discourses. This method has been recently employed by Julius Stone in his treatise *Legal Controls of International Conflict* (1954). It has appealed to me for my present purposes since it has permitted me to proceed in a straightforward manner with the main topics of the inquiry and at the same time to be reflective to a higher degree than conventional exposition would tolerate. The chapters are intended to provide a conventional analysis of the problems involved. The discourses are, at certain places, considerably divergent from the customary lines of philosophical expression. Especially in the Third, Fourth, and Fifth Discourses the reader may recognise the motifs of reasoning peculiar to psycho-analysis and related approaches. This feature of the discourses springs from my belief that concrete emotive, conative, and cognitive experiences of the inquirer are an essential ground of departure for inquiries such as those into the fundamental principles of justice. My concern with myself in relation to the present work in the discourses purports to be an effort to reach the ground of this concretum. On the other hand it is intended to represent also common tribulations of scholars likely to be met by them when they seek solutions to philosophical problems similar to those which constitute the theme of the present essay. The main purposes which the discourses are intended to serve can be described as follows: to gain positions and to clarify perspectives for the analyses in the chapters, to deal with doubts that emerge with respect to the methods and results of my inquiries, and to summarise the results of the preceding parts of the work.

My general efforts in this essay have been directed more to integration of existing views relating to the fundamental principles of justice than to a critical evaluation of these principles. Or it may be still more appropriate to say: I have tried to see a rather blurred picture of the fundamentals of justice presented by the contemporary doctrinal situation by means of a notional scheme compatible with this picture. I confess that I have also projected forms, shadings, and colours into this picture, retouched it at places, and perhaps even drawn my own lines within its blank portions.

First Discourse

I read that a man with his wife and three children was evicted by order of the court from a shabby dwelling because he was unable to pay the rent. He had been unemployed for some time, and his wife had been ill. The owner of the house is said to be a rich man, for whom the rent in arrears would mean only an addition to his already more than sufficient income. Neither of the parties is known to me, and I have never myself been in their situation. But I feel concerned. I ask whether the poor man was justly treated. He obviously thinks that he was not. And I wonder, does the landlord think in the same way? Presumably he believes that he obtained a just decision. Finally I ask, what is the attitude of the judge who made the eviction order? Most certainly he „apprehends“ that he did justice according to law[1].

This small incident brings wider issues to my mind. I deplore that some people live in misery while others live in extravagant luxury. And I deplore that racial discrimination, exploitation, and disabilities based on social status still exist in the world. These do not affect my personal life, but I feel concerned; I regret the injustice under which many people have to suffer, and I regret some people's idea of justice, so different from mine. This leads me to ask: Is there justice, and if there is, what is it? Can justice be known, and if it can, how? Ought justice to be done, and if it ought, when?

That there is no justice or that there is too little justice has been the complaint of men at all places and in all ages. They have longed for absolute justice[2], and hoped that the reign of justice would come in some future time. But such a longing and such a hope have never been

---

[1] For the meaning of this phrase see R. Pound: Justice according to Law, 1951, esp. Part. 3.

[2] See H. Kelsen: What Is Justice? 1957, 24.

fulfilled, nor is their fulfilment in sight. Justice has been regarded as something inseparable from our worthwhile existence, so that Kant was tempted into saying: „... if justice perishes, it is no longer of value for men to live on the earth[3]“. In spite of a quite universal agreement on the importance of justice and a quite universal craving for it, men still continue to suffer the horrors of its absence, and there are many who appear not to care about justice, or who oppose the efforts to realise it. But nobody, not even the most unjust man, appears to love injustice as something desirable in itself, or wants to be a victim of it. Why man is not or cannot be just permits of no simple answer. His indifference, his self-love, his „value-blindness[4]“ may account for it, but also his ignorance about what justice is, what is its worth, and what he ought to do to be just. And it may even be that in some cases there is a reason to believe that injustice is preferable to justice.

My own concern with justice is of long standing. I have suffered injustice, and have felt remorse for having failed to do justice to others; I have met with what I have considered just, and tried to be just to others; I have read, written, and pondered on the problem of justice. The problem has fascinated, haunted, and also perplexed me. In spite of all my lack of clarity about justice some notion of it has yet been in my mind, helping me to adopt viewpoints when the socially desirable and undesirable was involved, and enabling me to orient myself in various legal problems. An unstructured (preconceptual) notion of justice has had occasion to arise in my mind when I was confronted with situations which required regulation through agreements or commands. On these occasions I have found that the just is closely connected with the legal but not identical with it.

The unstructured notions of justice with which lawyers and other people mostly operate are mere intuitions and liable to be subjective, if not arbitrary. Such notions may be sufficient to settle a number of individual cases in a plausible way, but they lack the universal applicability which would enable one fruitfully to discuss justice and to take rational measures for its realisation. To arrive at universally applicable notions of justice, a comprehension of its content and demarcation of the range of the objects that it embraces is required. This means bringing intuitions of justice to the level of concepts.

There are two sciences preëminently concerned with what is just and with what is unjust: legal science and political science. But neither of these appears to be competent to inquire into the problems of the essence, existence, and worth of justice, which appear to be fundamental principles lying beyond the scope of any specific region of the Given. Legal and political sciences work with the notion of justice as something presupposed, as geometry works with the notion of the point, and as the

---

[3] See Kant: Die Metaphysik der Sitten, 1797, 139: „... *wenn die Gerechtigkeit untergeht, so hat es keinen Wert mehr, daß Menschen auf Erden leben.*“

[4] On this notion see G. Radbruch: Rechtsphilosophie, 4th ed. 1950, 91 ff.

natural sciences work with the notion of cause. This suggests that „justice" is a so-called basic notion of the legal and political sciences. Basic notions are not defined by the discipline whose basic notions they are, but by a pre-ordinated discipline of it. But what would be such a discipline? Analysis and definition of the notion of justice seems to require consideration of fundamental principles of justice, and these are circumstances lying beyond the scope of any theory of a specific region of the Given.

These considerations make me believe that the problem of the clarification of the notion of justice should be relegated to philosophy, the concern of which is to penetrate to the first principles of what is given. But what is philosophy[5]? It seems that philosophy as a single homogeneous discipline does not exist. There appear to be only philosophies, following different streams of thought and often being basically divergent from each other. In wanting to tackle a philosophical problem, I seem to have to decide in favour of one of them, or to construct my own „philosophy" for carrying out my inquiries into the fundamental principles of justice.

To decide in favour of one particular philosophical conception, doctrine, or system, is I feel excluded to me. This would mean for me an intolerable bias. All philosophical conceptions, doctrines, and systems have arisen from special historical and cultural situations which I might or might not share, and they all appear to be affected with faults which I do not want to admit into my inquiry. But to create a completely independent philosophical system of my own for my present purposes would mean a too ambitious and even an impracticable undertaking. Thus my proper course of action seems to be to link my work somehow with existing currents of philosophical thought. Even though I am not compelled to follow any particular current, I must at least try to preserve a continuity with the existing philosophical tradition by evaluating the contents of several philosophical conceptions, and by modifying and consolidating them to form a base for my special inquiries.

Despite the number of philosophies that exist and their frequently questionable value, there appears still to be something common to them all, something which permits an attempt to determine the meaning of the word „philosophy". Philosophical activity is, like the scientific, an activity whose aim is to obtain assured knowledge. „Philosophy" is a name used to designate this activity or the results of it. Philosophy, in common with the practical pursuits of men, strives for knowledge to promote the attainment of the ends which men set for themselves. In common with science, philosophy has a strictly methodical approach

[5] On the problem, What is philosophy?, see S. Alexander: Space, Time, and Deity, 3rd impr. 1950, vol. I, pp. 1–5; A. N. Whitehead: Science and the Modern World, 12th impr. 1953, 173–194; G. E. Moore: Some Main Problems of Philosophy, 1953, 1–27; K. Jaspers: Philosophie und Wissenschaft, 1949, passim; E. Fechner: Rechtsphilosophie, 1956, 1–7.

to problems and the search for reasons which would substantiate its propositions. In common with theology, philosophy is concerned with the ultimate reasons and ends of human life, with the origin of what exists, and with the ultimate realities and values. The essential difference between practical activity and philosophy is that in practical activity knowledge is sought for the attainment of various particular aims such as comfort and beauty, whereas in philosophy knowledge is ultimately sought for the attainment of a sole decisive comprehensive aim: understanding of all that is there. The essential difference between science and philosophy is that scientific knowledge is particular, extending only over limited parts of the knowable, whereas the entity which philosophy strives to apprehend is the All. The essential difference between theology and philosophy is that theology accepts certain statements (dogmas) as unquestionably true, whereas for philosophy there is nothing unquestionable.

One specific concern of philosophy is to provide fundamental notions that would constitute a basic matrix for inquiries into particular regions of the Given. This is the task of ontology[6]. Another specific concern of philosophy is to inquire into the principles of knowledge and to determine the conditions of its truth. This is the task of epistemology. A further specific concern of philosophy is to furnish instruments of methodical thinking and to determine the conditions of consistency of thought. This is the task of logic. Finally, philosophy is specifically concerned with the clarification of the problem of values. This task has been traditionally performed by ethics and aesthetics. It is appropriate to recognise a wider scope to philosophy's concern with values under the heading of axiology. These specific concerns of philosophy or philosophical disciplines, being different ways of approaching the same entity: the All, are all interrelated and are necessary for each other in the fulfilment of their particular tasks. But limited objects of knowledge, if they are viewed in the light of ultimate generalities can also be subjected to ontological, logical, epistemological, and axiological inquiries. In this way regional philosophies[7] such as philosophy of nature, legal philosophy, and philosophy of religion arise. To inquire into the fundamentals of justice is to investigate a regional-philosophic problem, namely a problem of political philosophy, which has for its preordinated disciplines all the above mentioned four main disciplines of philosophy.

---

[6] Cf. P. Tillich: Love, Power and Justice, 1954, 19, who characterises ontology as follows: „The questions of ontology are: ‚What does it mean that something *is?* What are the characteristics of everything *that participates in being?*‘" Cf. also W. Van Orman Quine: From a Logical Point of View, 1953, 1, who says that the ontological problem can be put in the simple words: „What is there?"

[7] On the concept of region in philosophy see E. Husserl: Ideas: General Introduction to Pure Phenomenology (transl. by W. R. Boyce Gibson, 1931) 77: „Region is just the *highest and most exclusive generic unity belonging to a concretum,* that is, the essential unitary connection of the *summa genera* which belong to the lowest differences within the concretum." See also ibid. 64.

The aims of philosophic knowledge are high. The attempt to apprehend the totality of everything, to determine the first principles of the All, to understand being-insofar-as-it-is-being[8], appears to be nothing short of impossible. This does not mean, however, that such attempts are necessarily idle. In philosophy, as elsewhere, complete and absolutely certain knowledge appears to be unattainable. Yet it seems that by striving for total understanding as for an ideal we may hope to achieve valuable intermediate ends. These intermediate ends are: more reliable knowledge, a more circumspective choice of principles of action, and more reasoned judgments. In these respects it can be hoped that the present inquiry into the fundamentals of justice should help towards a clearer thinking about justice, towards more enlightened action for the realisation of justice, and towards a better understanding of what is involved and what ought to be done when justice comes into conflict, for example, with truth, mercy, or utility.

It is, of course, obvious that in view of the unlimited scope of philosophic knowledge, even very restricted problems of philosophy cannot be expected to find their full elaboration in a limited work. Every philosophical notion appears to require for its full clarification more fundamental and comprehensive insights than an inquiring mind can possess. Philosophic activity, being an eternally unfulfillable aspiration to understand the All, involves a constant process of construction of notions. On the other hand, it involves a constant process of destruction of notions and the replacement of what is destroyed by what appears to be more solid in the given intellectual situation. Construction, destruction, and replacement of philosophical notions are involved also in the present inquiry. Any contribution of mine will most certainly suffer a similar fate in due course.

I. Preliminary Considerations

1. The Notion of Justice in Language

To obtain an unstructured (preconceptual) notion of justice as an heuristic basis for subsequent inquiries, it is appropriate first to consider the linguistic aspect of justice. Language is „the house of Being[9]"; there are insights in language, even wisdom, which should not be neglected by the inquirer in his search for proper meanings of words. The words „justice" and „just" have a rather wide range of application in English, as the corresponding words have in other languages[10]. An examination of these applications should give preliminary information about the meanings of the said words.

---

[8] For this expression see Tillich, op. cit. 18.

[9] A metaphoric phrase used by Martin Heidegger in his essay: Über den Humanismus, 1949, 5.

[10] On the equivocation of the word „justice" see R. Pound: Justice according to Law, 1951, 2 ff.; G. Del Vecchio: Justice (ed. by A. H. Campbell, 1952), 1 ff.

The principal contexts in which „justice“ occurs in English are represented in the following phrases: 1. „To do justice“, „to realise justice“, in which „justice“ means a social situation. 2. „The justice of a decision“, „There is no justice in this law“, in which „justice“ means a quality of a legal enactment. 3. „Administration of justice“, in which „justice“ means law. 4. „To bring a criminal to justice“, in which „justice“ means punishment inflicted by law. 5. „Natural justice“, in which „justice“ means certain procedural principles applied in courts. 6. „Mr. Justice X“, in which „justice“ means a person authorised to hold courts, to try cases, and to apply law. 7. „To complain with justice“, in which „justice“ means what is right, properly motivated, well-grounded.

As the above applications of the word „justice“ show, it is used also in a figurative sense. The word as it occurs in „Mr. Justice X“, „natural justice“, „administration of justice“, „to complain with justice“, and „to bring a criminal to justice“ appears to be a paranym. Only in the phrases of groups 1. und 2. does „justice“ seem to occur in a specific, and presumably in its proper, sense.

The principal contexts in which the adjective „just[11]“ occurs in English are: 1. „A just man“, „a just judge“, in which „just“ means a moral quality of a person. 2. „Just conduct“, „a just punishment“, „a just law“, in which „just“ means a quality of a social circumstance. 3. „A just price“, „a just reward“, in which „just“ means a quality of a value (in the objective sense). 4. „A just cause“, „a just excuse“, in which „just“ means a quality of certain legal facts. 5. „A just indignation“, „a just estimate“, „a just proportion“, „a just observation“, in which „just“ means a quality of various circumstances other than those specified above. Whether or not „just“ occurs in a figurative sense in some of the above phrases is *prima facie* not clear. Therefore it is to be considered whether „just“ is a necessary adjective in all these contexts.

It seems that a) in the phrases „a just man“ and „a just judge“; „just conduct“, „a just punishment“, and „a just law“; „a just price“ and „a just reward“ — the word „just“ cannot be replaced by any word which would strictly be a synonym of it. Substitution of „just“ with another word without affecting the meaning of the phrase in which it occurs seems to be possible, however, b) in the phrases „a just cause“ and „a just excuse“ (which in most cases are equivalent to „a lawful cause“ and „a lawful excuse“), „a just indignation“ (which ordinarly is equivalent to „a well-grounded indignation“), „a just proportion“ (which normally is equivalent to „a right proportion“), and „a just observation“ (which is equivalent to „a proper observation“). That „just“ in the phrases of group b) is not indispensable is corroborated by compara-

[11] It should be remarked that „just“ may be used also as an adverb. The adverbial meanings of the word are, however, without any direct connection with the word „justice“ and are of little interest for the present inquiry. The adverb corresponding to the noun „justice“ is „justly“.

tive philology. Thus in German (which is an Indo-European language like English) „just" is rendered as *„gerecht"* (a word corresponding to *„Gerechtigkeit"*, meaning „justice") in the phrases of group a), but with different words (*„rechtmäßig"* and *„richtig"*) in the phrases of group b). The same is the case in Estonian (which is not an Indo-European language), where the corresponding words are *„õiglane"* („justice" in Estonian is *„õiglus"*) on the one hand, and *„õiguslik"* and *„õige"* on the other.

The linguistic origin of the English words „justice" and „just" is Latin[12]. Their Latin equivalents *„iustitia"* und *„iustus, -a, -um"* had a wide range of meanings even in the classical period of this language[13], and so would be of little help for determining the proper or basic meanings of the words in question. What may be, however, significant for the present inquiry is that *„iustitia"* appears to be a derivation of *„ius"*, meaning „law"[14] or „right" (in the juristic sense). It is interesting to note that in other European languages in which the words signifying the notion of justice are not of Latin origin, these words are also derivations of the words signifying the juristic notions of law and right. Thus in German *„Gerechtigkeit"* is manifestly a derivation of *„Recht"*, in Russian *„pravilnost"* of *„pravo"*, and in Estonian *„õiglus"* of *„õigus"*. This suggests that there is an essential connection between men's intuitions of justice and law. Where the meanings of „justice" and „just" have no essential connection with law and rights, there is a reason to suspect that these are improper uses of the words „justice" and „just".

The above considerations lead to the conclusion that the meanings of the word „justice" which should be of a particular concern in this essay are „a social situation" and „a quality of a legal enactment". The meanings of the word „just" which are relevant for the present purposes are „a moral quality of a person", „a quality of a social circumstance", and „a quality of a value (in the objective sense)".

2. The Lawyer's Notion of Justice

The connection between the notions of justice and law indicated by the above linguistic analysis suggests that those who should know what justice is, are lawyers. Therefore the next step in the present attempt to obtain a notion of justice is to seek some acquaintance with

---

12 On the linguistic origin of *„iustitia"* Del Vecchio, op. cit. 3 ff., n. 8, gives some information.

13 See Ch. T. Lewis and Ch. Short: A Latin Dictionary, sub voce „justitia". See also ibid. „justus" and „justum".

14 Cf. the dictum of Ulpianus in D. 1, 1, 1: *„Iuri operam daturum prius nosse oportet, unde nomen iuris descendat, est autem a iustitia appellatum: nam, ut eleganter Celsus definit, ius est ars boni et aequi."* Cf. also the gloss to this dictum: *„Est autem ius a iustitia, sicut a matre sua, ergo prius fuit iustitia quam ius."* To hold this view, Ulpianus and his glossator could not have been philologists.

their views and attitudes with respect to justice. It might be expected that there is a typical lawyers' doctrine of justice, and that their juristic acumen has achieved a considerable penetration into the notions of justice and just.

However, this expectation is not borne out by the actual state of affairs. Although the words „justice" and „just" are not infrequently used in legal contexts, they often occur here as equivalent to „law" and „legal" (as, for example, in the phrases „administration of justice", „with just cause", and „without just excuse"). When „justice" and „just" and their opposites are used by lawyers in a different sense (as, for example, in the phrases „natural justice", „unjust enrichment", and „unjust benefit[15]"), they rarely attempt to define these notions in the contexts in which the words occur[16]. It appears that lawyers generally feel incompetent in the quest for justice, and participate in efforts to formulate and realise its idea only hesitantly or not at all[17]. As Erik Wolf rightly observes[18], legal studies and actual experiences gained in legal practice tend to create the impression of multiplicity[19], relativity and practical worthlessness of ideas such as that of justice. Hence many lawyers regard the arriving at universally acceptable concepts and criteria of justice as impossible and strive only for legally correct decisions. The popular definitions of justice, as well as the politicians' high sounding phrases and platitudes about it, are despised by lawyers as incompatible with the moral integrity of the legal profession. Further, lawyers feel that to reflect on justice somehow shakes the intellectual basis of their calling. For every such reflection may seem somehow to set in doubt the assumptions on which their work rests and to subject

---

[15] See, for example, Lord Mansfield's judgment in Moses v. Macferlan, 1760, 2 Burr. 1005, at 1012: „... the defendant ... is obliged by the ties of natural justice ... to refund the money." W. R. Anson: Principles of English Law of Contract (20th ed. by J. L. Brierly, 1952), 430: „A has received money which is just that he should pay over to B." See also A. H. F. Lefroy: The Basis of Case Law, 1906, 22, Law Quarterly Review, 293, at 299, passim; G. C. Cheshire and C. H. S. Fifoot: The Law of Contract, 4th ed. 1956, esp. 548–556.

When the term „just" is employed in the text of constitutions, its sense is particularly liable to transcend that of the term „legal". Constitutions are the fundamental law of a legal order and the words used in them can hardly derive their meaning from the law subordinate to the particular constitution. See for the occurrence of „just" in the Fifth Amendment of the United States Constitution („just compensation") and in Section 51 (xxxi) of the Australian Constitution („just terms"). See also for the occurrence of „justice" in Articles (1) and 2 (3) of the Charter of the United Nations.

[16] Cf. H. Winfield: Ethics in English Case Law, 1931/32, 45, Harvard Law Review, 112, at 118; R. Pound: The Ideal Element in American Judicial Decisions, ibid. 136, at 138.

[17] See E. Wolf: Rechtsgedanke und biblische Weisung, 1948, 12.

[18] See ibid. 12 ff.

[19] On the multiplicity of the idea of justice see E. N. Garlan: Justice and Legal Realism, 1941, 129.

their way of thinking, that is the legal method, to criticism of which they can make little use[20].

Although this may be the prevailing attitude of lawyers, there are outstanding exceptions which show that not all jurists have refrained from wondering about the fundamentals of justice, and that contributions to the clarification of the notion of justice have been made both by those who handle the practical side of law and by legal theorists.

Of the outstandig contemporary lawyers, the question. What is justice? was recently directly posed by Lord Denning, now one of the Lords of Appeal in England[21]. In trying to answer this question, he submits that justice is not something which can be seen; it is not temporal but eternal, not the product of man's intellect but of his spirit[22]. The nearest Lord Denning believes he can get to a definition of justice is that justice is „what the right-minded members of the community — those who have the right spirit within them, believe to be fair". This conception of justice places, he says, a great responsibility upon the lawyers. They represent the right-minded members of the community, and they can do what is fair between man and man and between man and the State only by means of just laws justly administered. That doing justice is the lawyer's task is implied in the words of the judicial oath, taken by every judge of England on his appointment. The guiding words of this oath „I will do right" mean „I will do justice", not „I will do law". Lord Denning points out that doing justice as the lawyer's task is implied also in the coronation oath of the Queen, whose delegates the judges are. The Archbishop asks: „Will you to your power cause Law and Justice, in Mercy, to be executed in all your judgments?" The Queen answers: „I will." In the coronation oath of the Queen, law and justice are treated as inseparable. This leads the learned judge to reproach some lawyers res caring too much for law and too little for justice. Instead of being, as they should be, men of spirit and vision making the law fit for the times in which we live, they become technicians, spelling out the meaning of words. In his view, the road to justice can be found only in those things which are right and true, not in relying overmuch on the technical rules of law. Lawyers setting out on the road to justice have two great objectives to achieve: to see that the laws are just and to

---

[20] The lawyer's attitude towards justice may be understood also on the ground that the notions „justice" and „just" do not belong to the same order as the typical lawyer's concepts, for example, „property", „contract", and „crime", but rather to the same order as „law", „duty", „legal relation", etc., which are the basic notions of legal science. To inquire systematically into these basic notions is the concern of legal philosophy, like systematic inquiry into the basic notions of natural sciences (for example, „cause", „space-time", „event") is the concern of philosophy of nature. The lawyer's reserve with respect to the problem of justice may thus be partly due to his aversion to transcend the limits of his science and to enter the domain of philosophy where he may feel a stranger.

[21] See A. Denning: The Road to Justice, 1955, 4—7 and viii.

[22] Cf. Lord Justice Morris: The Spirit of Justice, 1954, 13.

see that they are justly administered. Of these two objectives the latter is more important. The administration of justice depends on the quality of the men who are ready to undertake it.

What Lord Denning has said about justice is hardly a satisfactory answer to his question, What is justice? But it was not even his own hope to find such an answer[23]. He has set himself the more modest aim of clarifying to some extent the meaning of justice. His statements concerning what justice is appear to be as little complete and conclusive as were the corresponding statments of the great Roman lawyers. Thus the dicta, justice is „constant and perpetual will to accord everyone his law" (Ulpianus[24]) and justice is „the mind's disposition according everyone his due" (Cicero[25]) definitely do not satisfy the scholar's curiosity about what justice is. But they, like Lord Denning's statements, contain thoughts that the scholar may need for orientation in his search for a satisfactory answer. It may perhaps be expected that legal theorists, whose task it is to clarify the foundations of law, would deal more fully with the problem, What is justice? This expectation makes it appear worthwhile to outline the conceptions of justice of some outstanding contemporary writers on legal theory[26].

For Roscoe Pound[27], justice means a regime of social control to bring about and to maintain an ideal relation among men. In human nature, friction resulting from various drives of individuals is inherent. The task of social control is to conquer human nature by holding these drives in check, and thus to prevent dissolution and disruption of the group. Justice as an ideal relation[28] among men is an end or purpose of law, but it is not the only one. The ends of law include also morals in the sense of the ideal development of individual character, and security in the sense of assuring men freedom from aggression by others and good faith on the part of others in the general intercourse of society. To these

---

[23] He says the question, What is justice? „has been asked by men by far wiser than you and me and no one has yet found a satisfactory answer" (Denning, op. cit. 4).

[24] D. 1, 1, 10 pr.: *„Iustitia est constans et perpetua voluntas ius suum cuique tribuendi."*

[25] De Finibus 5, 23: *„... animi affectio suum cuique tribuens."*

[26] In the present section I propose to sketch the conceptions of justice of Roscoe Pound, Julius Stone, Hans Kelsen, and Vilhelm Lundstedt as typical academical lawyers' conceptions of justice. These writers might also be classed as legal philosophers whose doctrines of justice I shall consider in the last section of the present chapter. A reason for treating their thoughts under separate headings is that the former have approached the problem of justice from the direction of law whereas the latter have approached it from the direction of philosophy.

[27] For Roscoe Pound's conception of justice see his work: Justice according to Law, 1951, 1–35, esp. at 16, 19, 21, 28–31.

[28] The reason why Pound, in connection with justice, speaks of „an" ideal relation rather than of „the" ideal relation is that it is for him not a settled question what is *the* ideal relation as something ultimate and absolute. See ibid. 19.

ideas, justice stands in an antinomic relation. A satisfactory theoretical solution of this antinomy may prove impossible, but this does not force one to surrender to a „give-it-up philosophy", which holds that an ultimate theory of values cannot be found and that it is unscientific to seek to formulate values. Posing the question, What is the ideal relation among men?, Pound finds that a working idea — even if it is not convincingly ideal metaphysically, logically, or ethically — is one that should provide an acceptable answer to this question. With the guidance of this idea, experience developed by reason and reason tested by experience have taught men how to go a long way towards achieving the practical task of enabling men to live together. There has been a great variety of working ideas indicating what is an ideal relation among men. Thinkers have continually transcended the ideas offered by the past to more inclusive ideas. The inclusive idea to which Pound comes in search of an answer to his question is the idea of maximum satisfaction of human wants or expectations. Social control, preëminently law, has to reconcile and adjust these desires or wants or expectations so far as it can, in order to satisfy as many of them as it can.

According to Julius Stone[29], justice is a relation between wants, resources and outlets for dissatisfaction. This relation is a dynamic one: man's wants, for example, vary with the external environment and with his own psychological qualities and often fortuitous experience. A complete rational apprehension of justice is prevented by the emotive components in judgments as to its content. Irrespective, however, of non-rational features of justice, the idea of justice may still have great significance throughout social life. This significance indeed is presupposed by the very multiplicity of ideas of justice held by men, and the variability of these ideas in time. And, whatever the degree of success or failure of the search of men for justice, this search represents a social-psychological phenomenon of great importance, especially in modern democratic society. It sums up the attitude of constant criticism of existing law, and of unwillingness to accept law for the time being as more than only means to wider ends[30]. Although the content of justice seems relative, the very relativity of this content presupposes a constant base by reference to which this relativity is asserted. In social intercourse, which inevitably takes place in concrete socio-historical contexts, particular principles become crystallised by recourse to which situations are considered just or unjust. These principles are criteria of justice. The precepts specifying them are necessarily incomplete, being only attempts to determine the conditions of the realisation of the idea of justice in

---

[29] For Julius Stone's conception of justice see his treatises: The Province and Function of Law, 2nd ed. 1950, 212, 226, 296, 375, 778–785; Legal Controls of International Conflict, 1954, 50–56, esp. at 53 ff.

[30] See Stone: Province, 784. See there also a thought accredited by Stone to E. N. Garlan, Legal Realism and Justice, 1941, 127, 131, that justice is a „motive power", a „continuous prod to the asking and answering questions" and a thought that justice is the *set* and *constant purpose*, in one interpretation of Justinian's classical formula, to give each his due.

particular kinds of historical situations. The norms of positive law, the *de facto* demands and related ethical convictions supporting them, form parts of the empirical data from which criteria of justice may be drawn. Other parts (which may be even more decisive when there is a conflict) are found in conditions of society for the time being, in relation to their actual or potential satisfaction. On this view, the idea of justice as a standard of evaluation of law does not hover sublimely and apart above the facts of our actual societies, but is founded on a relationship among these facts. It follows from this conception of the criteria of justice that there is an irreducible minimum requirement of legal justice, without which adequate criteria could not emerge even in the particular time and place. This requirement is in a broad sense procedural: society ought to be so organised that men's felt wants can be freely expressed, and the law ought to protect that expression and even strive to provide it with channels through which it can compete ever more effectively for the support of politically organised society.

For Hans Kelsen[31], justice primarily means a possible, but not a necessary, quality of social order regulating the mutual relations of men. Secondarily it means a virtue of man. For a man is just if his behaviour conforms to the norms of social order supposed to be just. To say that a social order is just means that this order regulates the behaviour of men in a way satisfactory to all men, in other words, regulates it so that all men find their happiness in it. As long as the concept of happiness is defined in its original narrow sense of individual happiness (that is, man's happiness is what he himself considers it to be), there can be no order affording happiness to everyone: there can be no „just" order. For it is inevitable that the happiness of one individual will sometimes come into conflict with that of another. The happiness that a social order would be able to ensure can be happiness in the collective sense only, that means, the satisfaction of certain needs recognised by the social authority, the lawgiver, as needs worthy of being satisfied (such as the need to be fed, clothed, and housed). But the questions, which human needs are worthy of being satisfied, and especially what is their proper order of rank, cannot be answered by means of rational cognition. The decisions about such questions are value judgments, determined by emotional factors, and are therefore valid only for the judging subject; they are subjective in character; they are relative. The problem of value is primarily the problem of conflict of values. When there is no conflict of interests, there is no need for justice. The fact that there are certain values generally accepted in a certain society does not contradict the subjective and relative nature of these value judgments. That many individuals agree in their value judgments is no proof that these judgments are valid. The positive systems of values are always a result of the mutual influence that individuals exercise upon each other within a given group. Since humanity is divided into many nations, classes, religions, professions, etc., which

[31] For Hans Kelsen's conception of justice see his works: What Is Justice? 1957, 1–24 and: General Theory of Law and State, 1946, 3–14.

are often at variance with each other, there are a great many very different conceptions of justice: too many for one to be able to speak simply of „justice“. What absolute justice is for which mankind has been longing, Kelsen declares, he does not know. He acquiesces in a relative justice which for him is that social order under whose protection the search for truth can prosper. This justice, he says, is the justice of freedom, peace, democracy, and tolerance.

According to Vilhelm Lundstedt[32], the assertions that the lawmaker should be led by justice, and that the courts have to „administer justice“ (meaning: to realise justice), are empty phrases. They are not founded on facts, but are completely senseless. There is no justice. Neither is there any objective „ought“. The entire legal ideology — including legal rights and duties, wrongfulness and lawfulness — goes up in smoke. In its reasoning, jurisprudence is founded on value judgments. Such judgments state nothing whatsoever about reality. They are, therefore, neither true nor false. They differ from proper judgments, because they are dependent on the feelings of the person who makes the judgment. A purely theoretical examination (that is one which is completely freed from all emotional influences) only establishes facts, and could never lead to establishing that something ought to be done or that something is just. In value judgments there seems to be a reference to the thing itself, but actually only the conception of the thing is referred to. Justice-judgments, like all value judgments, are and remain an expression of a feeling of a value, and are consequently determined by each person's emotional attitude; they are subjective. They specify nothing about reality, and can never be true, never objective.

From the above views advanced by five distinguished contemporary lawyers a number of features of justice and the just essential for the present inquiry can be culled. These views suggest that justice is a relation, that it is something subjective, relative, something intimately connected with man's emotive life. The content of justice is indeterminate; therefore criteria of justice, or arbiters of justice (that is, rightminded members of the community who would say what is just in a particular case) are required to give justice an applicable meaning in a given situation. The just is a value and the statements relating to justice are value judgments. The above presented conceptions of justice do not appear to stand as isolated units of thought but to rely on more basic thoughts which would determine what is meant by words such as „right-minded“, „value“, „ought“, „statement“, „existence“, and „intellect“. The sense of these words is not elaborated even by the writers on legal theory but seems to be presupposed by them. So the above lawyers' conceptions of justice direct the inquirer's attention to philosophy. They invite him, first

[32] For Vilhelm Lundstedt's conception of justice see his essay: Law and Justice, in P. Sayre (ed.): Interpretation of Modern Legal Philosophies, 1947, 450—483. See also his work: Superstition or Rationality in Action for Peace? 1925, 33 ff., 129 ff., 189 ff.; and his treatise: Die Unwissenschaftlichkeit der Rechtswissenschaft, 1932, vol. I, pp. 171 ff.; 1936, vol. II, pp. 25 ff., 239 ff.

of all, to consider the views held on justice in the history of philosophy, in which „justice" has been an important theme throughout the ages. As philosophical thinking (and to a considerable extent even legal thinking) is a continuation of mythical thinking, it may be expected that certain beginnings of the philosopher's concern about justice lie in ancient mythology.

3. The Mythical Notion of Justice

That there is a connection between the intuitions of justice and law *(ius)* is suggested not only by linguistic data but also by Greek mythology, in which lie important roots of Western philosophical as well as of legal thought[33]. Tracing the notion of justice in Greek mythology, one finds that even the name Dike[34], the goddess of justice, indicates her intimate relation to law. To the range of meanings of the word „*δίκη*" belong „judicial decision", „law", „law-suit", and „an action of law[35]".

---

[33] There is a great concern with the idea of justice in Jewish-Christian religious writings. But this concern never takes the form of a mythical picture of justice clear in outlines and rich in details as Greek myths and dramas offer. It is doubtful as to whether the idea of justice as constituted in those religious writings relates to the same idea of justice which has been a subject of Western juristic and political interest. The continuity of the idea of justice as formed by Greek mythology with the idea of justice occurring in Western legal and political thought is, however, quite manifest.

[34] On the linguistic origin of the word „*δίκη*", Professor Jaan Puhvel has kindly supplied the following learned note:

„*δίκη* is historically equated with Sanskrit *diśā* („direction"); the root noun Skt. *diś*-corresponds to Latin **dix* in the set phrase *dicis causā* („for form's sake"). The underlying Indo-European verbal root **deiḱ-* means „to point out, show" (Skt. *diśáti,* Gk. *δείκνυμι,* Hittite *tekkušanu-,* Lat. *in-dicō,* Gothic *ga-teihan,* Old High German *zeigōn).* In Latin *dīcō* has assumed the secondary meaning „to say". *δίκη* thus may have meant earlier something like „proper direction". Note that the adjective *δίκαιος* in Homer means „observant of custom", and only later „righteous", „just" in both legal and moral sense. Thus the origins of the word *δίκη* are semantically close to the notion of „established rule, statute law".

From a strictly etymological point of view the origins of the words *δίκη* and *iūs* are, of course, disparate. In Latin *iūs,* denoting largely merely *iūs civīle* (opposition: *iūsque fāsque est),* is in origin an old sacral word cognate with Skt. *vós* („weal"), especially in the formulaic phrase *śam ca yóś ca* („hail and weal"), and with Avestan *yaož-dadāiti* („to purify ritually"). It meant in Old Latin (in the form *ious*) „religious formula having force of law" (cf. *iūra lēgēsque). iūdex* („judge") goes back to **ious-dix* („one who points to such formulae"). Such use of *ious* was specifically Latin, for the other Italic languages Oscan and Umbrian employed, corresponding in meaning to *ius,* a cognate to Lat. *modus* (Umbr. *mers* for *iūs,* Osc. *meddix* for *iūdex).* The verb *iūrāre* („to swear") was derived form *iūs* (cf. *iūsiūrandum* meaning „oath"), like *iustus,* which in turn yielded *iūstitia."*

[35] For the range of meanings of „*δίκη*" in the ancient Greek see H. G. Liddell and R. Scott: A Greek-English Lexikon, sub voce „*δίκη*".

In the Greek mythical conception, Dike was a daughter of the supreme deity Zeus[36] and of Themis[37], who was the deity of the binding order of the world and acted as adviser to Zeus. The father of Themis was Uranos, the god of the firmament, to whose nature belonged expansion and height. Her mother was Gaia, the goddess of the earth, to whose nature belonged firmness, form, and depth. Themis was of Titanic origin, but as the fostermother of Zeus, and after the *titanomachia* as a wife of Zeus, she stood close to the Olympic gods. With Zeus, Themis begot also Eirene, the goddess of peace; Eunomia, the goddess of welfare („good state"); and Tyche, the goddess of unknown („hidden") fate. Dike gave a virgin birth to Hesychia, the goddess of serenity („stillness resting in itself").

The antagonists of Dike were Eris, the goddess of strife; Hybris, the goddess of excess and distortion; and the daughters of Eris: Dysnomia, Lethe, and Amphilogiai. Dysnomia, the deity of disorder („bad constitution"); Lethe, the deity of forgetfulness and concealment; and Amphilogiai, the deities of false and ambiguous words, were fatherless like Eris herself, having arisen directly out of the essence of their mother, who was born from Nyx, the deity of darkness. The helpers of Dike, apart from her sisters Eirene and Eunomia, were Styx, Nemesis, Erinyes, and Praxidikai. Styx, the Titanic god of gloom and depth was the punisher of unpardonable violations of law, such as perjury was for the Greeks. Nemesis, a sister of Eris, was the rectifier who punished equal wrongdoing with equal measures and unequal wrongdoing with unequal measures. Erinyes, who were daughters of Gaia and half-sisters of Themis, were goddesses of revenge. They acted as the guardians of the sacred law and mercilessly persecuted the offenders of this law, punishing them with death. Praxidikai, who were daughters of Zeus and half-sisters of Dike, were deities of the execution of law. They carried out punishment imposed by Dike.

---

[36] As a curiosity it may be mentioned that Grotius has suggested (De Jure Belli ac Pacis, Proleg., 12) that the Latin „ius" is of the same linguistic origin as „Zeus" („Iovis", „Iupiter"), which would imply that justice is an emanation of the Supreme Ruler of the Universe, whose one aspect is binding order („*iugum*", „*iungere*" derived from the same roots as the Sanskrit „*yu*", which means „to bind"). If it is considered that in the early conception law was a divine order, an expression of God's will, one can find the confirmation of the intimate connection of the notions of justice and law even in Jewish-Christian monotheistic religions, in which justice is regarded as an attribute of God Himself, connoting the „infallible proportion and intrinsic harmony of His Will". Cf. G. Del Vecchio: Justice (ed. by A. H. Campbell, 1952), 5. On the idea of justice in the Holy Scriptures, see H. Kelsen: What Is Justice? 1957, 25–81.

[37] For a detailed description of the relations of Dike to other Greek deities see E. Wolf: Griechisches Rechtsdenken, 1950, vol. I, pp. 19–69. See also for references to relevant literature and sources there. And see H. Kelsen: Society and Nature, 1943, 196–199, 356 ff.

The relations of Dike to the above deities suggest that, in the Greek mythical conception, justice is distinguished from the binding order of the world and from good councel. It is also distinguished from peace, welfare, unknown fate, and serenity. It is, however, close to all of them. The Greek mythology also suggests that justice is distinct from due punishment, retribution, and execution of law, which are, however, accessory to it. In the Greek mythical conception, justice is further regarded as opposed to strife, excess and distortion, disorder, forgetfulness and concealment, falsity, deceitfulness, and ambiguity.

To complete the present sketch of the mythical conception of justice, it is to be noted that Dike was conceived in Greek mythology[38] as a deity who created order, who guided, illumined, rectified, demanded, fought, and helped. As a deity who created order, Dike maintained the binding order established by Themis necessary for the existence of society. As a deity who guided, Dike took care that the maintained order was a good order, that is, an order under which peace, welfare and well-being prevailed in the community. As a deity who illumined, Dike, like Aletheia (the goddess of truth), brought light into the darkness of man's endeavours; she made visible what was obscure in social life so that it could be judged according to the divine design of the world. As a deity who rectified, Dike imposed obligations on everyone to live in accordance with his nature or to atone for failure to do so. As a deity who fought, Dike was in constant struggle with Eris and Hybris as well as with the daughters of Eris, to prevent strife, excess, distortion, concealment, and ambiguity from prevailing. In contrast to the precepts of Themis, Dike's commands were not indisputable and inviolable. There was always a possibility of misunderstanding or of contesting them so that in a dispute each party could believe in and call on Dike being on his side. As a deity who helped, Dike never had favourites[39]. But she aided those seeking their rights, and accorded to them their due at some time in the future, which due they were to receive then from Tyche, the deity of unknown fate, a sister of Dike.

These characteristics of Dike are what constitute *δικαιοσύνη*, an abstraction which, under the names of *„iustitia"*, *„justice"*, *„Gerechtigkeit"*, *„giustizia"*, etc., has played an important role in Western philosophical, legal, and political thought. If *δικαιοσύνη*, the essence of Dike, can be summarised in a few words, it may be said that it is lawfulness under right, reasonable, divine precepts, which precepts are, however, not indisputable and inviolable. It imports a dynamic principle of social balance to be achieved by struggle, circumspection, reliance on the existing (that is, preserving continuity), solicitude, and concern. In short, justice in the Greek mythical conception imports a principle of behaviour which can be expressed by the English word „care" and by the Latin word *„cura"*.

---

[38] See Wolf, op. cit. 39–45.

[39] This is why the goddess of justice is depicted her eyes bound.

4. The Notion of Justice in Philosophy

The philosophical use of the word „justice" *(„δίκη")* appears for the first time in Western recorded thought in Anaximander's mysterious dictum saying that the Boundless *(ἄπειρον)* is „where existing things arise and also perish, according to necessity; for they do justice and make reparation to one another for their injustice, according to the arrangement of time[40]". A related thought occurs in Parmenides, whose one dictum contains the thought that birth and destruction are held in bounds by justice[41]. The Anaximandrean and Parmenidean dicta suggest that these sages conceived justice as an *ἀρχή* of cosmological import, a principle regulating the operation of the forces of nature on the elements of the world[42]. Another early philosophical use of the word „*δίκη*" occurs in Herakleitus who, by saying that „to God all things are beautiful, good, and just whereas men regard some things as just, others as unjust[43]", seems to point out that men's distinction of justice and injustice is due to their limited understanding. In this dictum there is also a suggestion that justice is something relative, a thought later developed by the sophists, in whose political arguments it figured as the central issue[44].

The use of the word „*δίκη*" in the dicta of Anaximander, Parmenides, and Herakleitus is significant as the known beginning of Western speculation about justice. None of them, however, appears to have had any direct influence on the Platonic and Aristotelian doctrines, in which Greek thought on justice reached its culmination. These doctrines had their origin in the Pythagorean philosophy, for which the principle of justice was characterised by the idea of retaliation *(τὸ ἀντιπεπονθός)*. The Pythagoreans conceived justice as equality, namely as correspondence between opposite terms, and compared it with a

---

[40] See H. Diels: Die Fragmente der Vorsokratiker, 5th ed. 1934, 89, fragm. 1. For interpretations of the dictum of Anaximander see M. Heidegger: Holzwege, 2nd ed. 1950, 296–343; E. Wolf: Griechisches Rechtsdenken, 1950, vol. I, pp. 218–234; W. Jaeger: Paideia: the Ideals of Greek Culture (transl. by G. Highet, 1939), 157 ff.

[41] See Diels, op. cit., 236, fragm. 8, lines 13–15: „ . . . justice does not allow [being] either to be born or destroyed by releasing it from bonds, but holds [it]."

[42] See B. Russell: History of Western Philosophy, 1946, 46. On the cosmological concept of justice of the Ionian school see J. Burnet: Greek Philosophy, 1928, Part I, p. 28 ff. On the idea of justice in pre-Sokratic philosophy as importing the principle of retribution see H. Kelsen: Society and Nature, 1943, 233–248.

[43] See Diels: op, cit. 173, fragm. 102. For an interpretation of this dictum see Wolf, op. cit. 254–259. On the Herakleitean conception of justice see also Burnet, op. cit. 61 ff.

[44] On the sophists' legal and political thought see E. Wolf: Griechisches Rechtsdenken, 1952, vol. II, pp. 9–171.

square number: it gives the same back for the same, and thus is the same multiplied by the same[45].

In the Platonic doctrine, justice is conceived as an ethical principle[46]. It is conceived as a universal virtue regulative of the whole individual and social life. For Plato the essence of justice lies in doing one's task *(τὰ ἑαυτοῦ πράττειν)*, be this task the development of the faculties belonging by nature to every part of the soul or to every social class. As a regulative principle, justice harmonises actions assigning them proper direction and proper functions. Among the virtues, it has a special place because it assigns to other virtues such as wisdom, courage, and temperance, their proper role in the organic whole of the individual and of society.

Aristotle, like Plato, conceives justice as a virtue, that is as an ethical principle[47]. Virtue is defined by Aristotle as a mean state *(μεσότης)* between two extremes, which are vices. He distinguishes justice in a particular and in a general sense. In the general sense, justice means lawfulness, that is, conformity to positive law. In the particular sense, justice means right proportion, which is a *mesótes* between too much and too little. There are two kinds of particular justice: distributive and synallagmatic[48]. The precept of distributive justice is „To everyone according to his deserts!", that is, „Equal shares to equal persons and unequal shares to unequal persons"! This principle is applied in public life, and it governs the giving of honour, wealth, and other divisible assets of the community. The principle of synallagmatic justice is equality of what is given and what is received. It applies to civil transactions and civil wrongs.

The mediaeval Christian philosophers retained a continuity with the conceptions of justice elaborated by Plato, Aristotle, and the Stoics, but framed it on the basis of their metaphysical and religious ideas. Thus St. Augustine[49] considers the essence of justice to consist

---

[45] On the Pythagorean conception of justice see G. Del Vecchio: Justice (ed. by A. H. Campbell, 1952), 42—50; A. Verdross-Drossberg: Grundlinien der antiken Rechts- und Staatsphilosophie, 2nd. ed. 1948, 26—29; Kelsen, op. cit. 360 ff.

[46] On the Platonic conception of justice see H. Kelsen: What Is Justice? 1957, 82—109; Verdross-Drossberg, op. cit. 69—126; B. Horvath: Die Gerechtigkeitslehre des Sokrates und des Platon, 1931, 10, Zeitschrift für öffentliches Recht, 258—280. The relevant Platonic dialogues are Politeia and Nomoi.

[47] For the Aristotelian conception of justice see Aristotle: The Nicomachean Ethics (transl. by H. Rackham, 1947), bk. v. For the Aristotelian conception of virtue see ibid., bk. ii.

On the Aristotelian doctrine of justice see M. Hamburger: Morals and Law, 1951, passim, esp. 33—110; M. Solomon: Der Begriff der Gerechtigkeit bei Aristoteles, 1937; Kelsen: What Is Justice? 110—136.

[48] The latter is called by Aristotle also rectificatory, corrective, equalising, or bilateral justice.

[49] For the Augustinian concept of justice see St. Augustine: De Diversis Questionibus, esp. ch. xxxi. On his legal and political thought see J. Sauter: Die philosophischen Grundlagen des Naturrechts, 1932, 57—65.

in love of the highest good, that is, in love of God. The idea of justice is embodied in natural law *(lex naturalis)*, which is the transcription of eternal law *(lex aeterna)*, the divine reason and will, in the soul of man. With some hesitation, St. Augustine says: an unjust[50] law is not a law *(Mihi lex esse non videtur, que justa non fuerit)*. No hesitation concerning the relation of law and justice occurs in St. Thomas Aquinas[51], in whose doctrine the Aristotelian conception of justice finds a glorious elaboration through scholastic method on the basis of mediaeval theology. He declares that unjust laws do not bind in conscience[52]. This thought is frequently expressed in the phrase „*lex injusta non est lex*". Binding law according to St. Thomas is an irradiation of the eternal law, which is divine truth itself; it is an enunciation of reason, and it is just. Justice is conceived by him as that principle of eternal law which determines the relation of one man to another and the share which a man is obligated to accord to another.

The philosophical conceptions of justice belonging to the modern age show a tendency towards emancipation from religious ideas, even though metaphysical notions continue to be employed in them. As a typical example of the transition from the mediaeval to the contemporary conceptions, the doctrine of justice offered by Leibniz may be mentioned[53]. Leibniz conceives justice as *caritas sapientis*, that is, the virtue which directs love to the goal of the universal good. There are three degrees of justice: universal, distributive, and commutative, which are all characterised by correspondence and proportionality. The precept of universal justice *(pietas vel probitas)* is „Live honestly!"; it is applied in the religious community. The precept of commutative justice *(ius strictum)* is „Harm no one!"; it is applied in the family community. The precept of distributive justice *(aequitas)* is „Accord everyone his due!"; it is applied in the civil community. According to Leibniz the duties following from justice are absolutely valid. They refer to the universal order and exist even where there is no one to enforce them.

In contemporary legal and political philosophy the themes found in the classical doctrines of justice have variously been taken up and developed on the basis of the philosophical conceptions current in our time. As typical of the present doctrinal situation, the conceptions of justice proffered by Jean Dabin, Giorgio Del Vecchio, Gustav Radbruch, and Barna Horvath will be outlined here.

---

[50] See St. Augustine: De Libero Arbitrio, ch. i, 5.

[51] For the conception of justice of St. Thomas Aquinus see his treatise Summa Theologica, II–II, 58, 79, 80, 122. On his legal and political thought see Sauter, op. cit. 70–83. See also C. J. Friedrich: Die Philosophie des Rechts in historischer Perspektive, 1955, 25–30.

[52] See St. Thomas Aquinus: Summa Theologica, I–II, 96–4.

[53] For the conception of justice in Leibniz see esp. his works: Nova Methodus Discendae Docendaeque Jurisprudentiae, Part II; Dissertatio I de Actorum Publicorum Usu ..., §§ 11, 12, 13. For discussion of the relevant thoughts in Leibniz and for further references see Del Vecchio, op. cit. 25–27, 39 ff.; Sauter, op. cit. 98–104.

According to Jean Dabin[54], justice in the widest sense merges with morality. In this sense it corresponds to the fulfilment of all duties prescribed by honesty in the private life of the individual and in social life. In the strict sense, justice means the virtue which attributes everyone his right (or dignity). Unlike prudence, moderation, and fortitude, which are related to the very person whose passions they regulate and measure, the function of justice is to order the conduct of man in matters relative to another. Justice equalises the attitude of the subject to what is the rigorous right of another individual or of collectivity. This right is for its holder „his own" *(suum),* and he may exact respect for it by force. In contrast to moderation and fortitude, justice rectifies, measures, and proportions the „outward operation", in other words, what is outside of any consideration of dispositions relating to the debtor. It does not simply harmonise antagonistic interests but gives to each of the given interests *what is due* to it, neither more nor less. In this consists the „just or golden mean" peculiar to the virtue of justice. There are three kinds of justice: commutative, distributive, and legal. In commutative justice, equality is determined as a thing to thing, that is, the creditor of justice has a right to what belongs to him simply because the thing is *his* irrespective of what his personal quality may be. In distributive justice equality is proportionate to the dignity (or the rank) which a person has as a member of a society. Since the ranks in society are not equal, the „mean" in distributive justice is taken according to the proportion of things to persons, so that the person who is superior in rank is entitled to more than is another person who is of inferior rank. In legal justice equality is proportionate to the common good. Here the holder of the right is the State. The debtors of legal justice are the private individuals and groups who are bound, whatever their rank, to render the social whole what is due to it on the part of its members. The object of legal justice is „ordination for the common good". Law is not the creator of justice but confines itself to rendering the content of justice more precise according to contingencies. All these three kinds of justice leave a margin of indeterminacy, the widest being that of legal justice. It remains a matter of appraisal how the applications of even „given" concepts such as „public good", which determine the subject matter of justice, ought to pass into law.

Giorgio Del Vecchio[55] conceives justice as a necessary fundamental attitude of consciousness. The elements of justice are bilateralness, parity, reciprocity, requital and reward. Bilateralness is an essential of every juridical determination; it means that two subjects are placed

---

[54] For Dabin's conception of justice see his treatise: Théorie Générale du Droit, 1944, Part III, ch. ii, iii. Or see an English translation by K. Wilk of this work entitled: General Theory of Law published in colume IV of 20th Century Legal Philosophy Series, 1950, 22—470, the relevant pages being 434—441; 443—449, 466.

[55] For Del Vecchio's conception of justice see his work cited supra n. 45, pp. 77—221, esp. at 77—90.

on the same plane and linked with each other so that to one subject's claim corresponds the other subject's obligation. Parity means the initial equality of the subjects, which is presupposed among those participating in bilateral relations. Reciprocity means an inseparable correlation of the subjects. Through this correlation the affirmation of a personality is at the same time its limitation in respect of the personality of another affirmed in the same act. Requital means a virtual authorisation of the same act between the same subjects, supposing their roles are reversed. Reward means corresponding treatment of one subject by another based on the evaluation of every act in its objective significance. Concerning the relations of law and justice, Del Vecchio's view is that justness is not an essential of law: law can also be unjust. But justice endows law with its moral worth. To be just, law has to correspond to the nature of man which is characterised by the absolute superiority of the subject over the object.

According to Gustav Radbruch[56], justice is a value-standard of positive law. It is the objective which the lawmaker seeks but may fail to achieve. The just is an absolute, a basic value like the true, the good, and the beautiful; it is not derivable from any other supposedly higher value. It is necessary to distinguish: (1) justice as a virtue, that is, as a personal quality (for instance, a just judge) — this is subjective justice; (2) justice as a relation between men (for instance, a just price) — this is objective justice. Subjective justice is the attitude of mind directed to the realisation of objective justice. The former stands to the latter in the same relation as truthfulness does to truth. Consequently, objective justice is the primary, and subjective justice is the secondary form of justice. In objective justice Radbruch distinguishes: (a) justice as a conformity to positive law (legality), (b) justice as a pre- and translegal idea of law (justice in the narrow sense). The core of justice in the narrow sense is equality. Equality determines two forms of justice; commutative and distributive. Commutative justice means the absolute equality of service and counterservice. Distributive justice means proportional equality according to the deserts of persons. Legal equality in the sense of commutative justice presupposes a distributive act, namely a distribution of the same legal status to persons. Thus commutative justice is based on distributive justice. The latter is the original, and the former the derived form. The relation of justice (in the narrow sense) and law is determined by Radbruch as follows: „Law is the reality whose purpose is to serve justice[57].“ The fact that in a legal case justice may compete with equity does not, he claims, affect this definition, because equity is justice for the individual case. Justice is the specific principle of law,

[56] For Radbruch's conception of justice see his lectures published under the title: Vorschule der Rechtsphilosophie, 1947, 23—25, and his treatise: Rechtsphilosophie, 4th ed. 1950, 124 ff., 168—183. This work has been published in English translation in vol. IV of: 20th Century Legal Philosophy Series (transl. by K. Wilk, 1950), 47—22, the relevant pages being 107—120.

[57] See Radbruch: Rechtsphilosophie, p. 127: *„Recht [ist] die Wirklichkeit, . . . die den Sinn hat, der Gerechtigkeit zu dienen.“*

but it is not the exhaustive principle. It is only one aspect of the legal idea[58], whose other aspects are expediency *(Zweckmäßigkeit)* and legal certainty *(Rechtssicherheit)*. As these three principles can be in conflict with each other, the legal idea is of an antinomic character. These conflicts cannot be solved by philosophy. It is not the task of philosophy to remove the need for decisions but to confront man with decisions. Philosophy ought not to make life easy but problematic[59].

Barna Horvath[60] conceives justice as the specific value of social rightness. The basic idea of justice is that what is right in one case is right in every identical case. To apply different moral measures to identical cases is radical injustice. In comparison with morality, which means freedom and is irrational, subjective, and individual, justice is law-like, rational, objective, and general. However, the substance and source of the value of justice is morality. Justice has objectivity only as truth, but it has value only as morality. And only the objectivity, generality, rationality and law-likeness of morality is justice. Social rightness raises the problem to what extent the requirements of solitary morality may be followed as against the moral requirements followed by others in the environment of society. In this environment justice acts as the barrier and limit of morally right behaviour. As applied to society, which means coercion and mutual interference with behaviour, justice

---

[58] Cf. W. Sauer: Juristische Elementarlehre, 1944, 23, 65. Sauer conceives justice as one aspect of the legal idea, an idea that gives sense and value to the legal norms. The other aspect of the legal idea is common weal, which is justice realised. Justice, according to Sauer, is the highest aim of every juristic activity. It is a regulative idea — an aim which remains forever unattainable and veiled in mysterious obscurity, although it stands out clearer and clearer the more one proceeds to attain it.

[59] Radbruch's *ultima verba* bring two important modifications to his conception of justice. Because they do not seem to fit into the *system* of his thought on justice (which system was developed earlier), the outline in the present text has not included a statement of them. Towards the end of his life, Radbruch conceived the conflict between justice, legal certainty, and expediency as an *inner* tension, as a soliloquy of justice, rather than as a tension within the legal idea. He regarded this „inner tension" and the paradoxes resulting therefrom not as something ultimate but as something penultimate which is to be transcended by love. (See E. Wolf's Introduction to the 4th edition of Radbruch's: Rechtsphilosophie, p. 72). The other important point in which Radbruch modified his conception of justice concerned the relation of justice to law. His: Fünf Minuten Rechtsphilosophie (written in 1945 and published in the annex of the 4th edition of: Rechtsphilosophie, pp. 335—337) suggests that a normative order, to be law, must not only be oriented to justice but must itself be just to some degree. He says (p. 336) that there *can* be laws of such measure of injustice and social harmfulness that validity and even legal character must be denied to them.

[60] This account of Horvath's conception of justice is drafted on the basis of his Hungarian treatise: Outline of Theory of Law (A Jogelmèlet vàzlata) 1937, 86, 116—119. See also his treatise: Rechtssoziologie, 1934, 264 ff. and his article: Gerechtigkeit und Wahrheit, 1929, 4, Internationale Zeitschrift für Theorie des Rechts, 1—54.

means a measure diminishing wants, lessening coercion and suffering. It means a measure of increasing satisfaction of interest, a measure securing happiness and freedom made available by a specific social technique. It is a measure endorsed as relative moral rightness. The requirement of justice in society is actualisation of the greatest and, at the same time, the most equally distributed available happiness, freedom, and satisfaction of want. Since there is a tension between the abstract generality of justice and concrete individuality of morality, equity is needed to avoid the tension from which a dangerous conflict may result. Equity extenuates the rigidly strict thesis of justice according to direct promptings of morality. It is the channel through which the ever renewed substance of morality flows into the emptied blood vessels of justice. Seeking to determine the relation between justice and law, Horvath says that justice is the limit of the social availability of morality and freedom secured by law. It is the measure of freedom and mutuality not exceeding the performance of law. It does not demand anything that is beyond the law's capacity of performance[61].

The above outline of the conceptions of justice in philosophy reveals a certain continuity of thought about justice from its early Greek beginnings up to the present day. It also reveals that there is a considerable unity of the philosophical conceptions of justice with the linguistic, the lawyer's, and the mythical notions of justice. From the above sketch it may be apprehended that justice is characterised by an equality, a proportionality, and a correspondence; that it is a regulative principle of man's social conduct and attitudes, a principle which imports balance and limitation of this behaviour; that it is a virtue or an idea or a value; and that it stands in close connection with law, although it may not coincide with law.

The contexts in which the philosophical doctrines of justice are presented raise a number of philosophical problems of general nature but do not attempt to solve or clarify them. Such problems are, for example, What is relation?, What is idea?, What is value? It is thus obvious that the philosophical doctrines of justice, like lawyers' doctrines of justice, relegate the inquirer to insights which the basic disciplines of philosophy: ontology, epistemology, logic, and axiology — may supply.

Second Discourse

Having traced the notion of justice as embodied in language, legal thought, mythology, and philosophy, I may now ask how the results thus reached might be used as a guide for my further inquiries. An obvious way to proceed would be to try to discover common elements of various

[61] By the capacity of law's performance Horvath means „its ability to further or hinder by its development, the development of society and that of each social objectivisation, in various directions". From the capacity of law's performance the value quality of law may be inferred. See Horvath: A Jogelmèlet vàzlata, 86.

embodiments of the notion and then organise them into a whole representing what „justice“ means. But this procedure raises two doubts: First, do not skeptical or negative attitudes towards a determination of justice make any inquiry into the fundamentals of justice pointless? Second, is my survey of the various notions of justice complete enough to allow its use as a sufficient heuristic basis for the subsequent inquiry? Even if I could ascertain a number of common elements in a variety of *hic et nunc* existing notions of justice, the possibility is not excluded that their being such elements is due to the limited scope of my survey; any extension of the scope of my survey may remove any substantial common features of the notions examined and prove only the existence of their discrepancies.

The first doubt may be countered by the following consideration: In fact, none of the authors whose conceptions of justice were described above is entirely negative about justice. Even Lundstedt, although he says that there is no justice, operates with the words „justice“ and „just“ and signifies something by them. How else could the subjective and emotive character of justice be pointed out by him? And how else can he say that the justice-judgments do not specify anything about reality, and even that there is no justice?! Kelsen rightly emphasises that there is a great number of conceptions of justice and that they are at variance with each other[62]. However, the fact that people widely disagree in their views about justice seems no more to prove that all these views are untenable than an agreement about them would prove that they are tenable. From the variety of these views it does not follow conclusively that arriving at reasonable notions of justice is impossible or that all existing conceptions of justice are devoid of any significance for an inquiry into the fundamental principles of justice. There appears to be nothing in the way of construing a concept of justice from the elements of several discrepant views about it. Proceeding in that way I may not succeed in apprehending justice as something concrete, something founded on spatial-temporal facts. But why should justice not be an abstraction? Abstractions, such as numbers, geometrical figures, and principles of logic, also have some kind of existence, and may be even of considerable practical importance. Lundstedt, contending that there is no justice[63], obviously does not intend to say that justice has no existence whatsoever. What he is actually denying is that justice is there as a particular kind of entity, namely as an entity that exists in space-time[64]. In this I can agree with Lundstedt: the characteristic features of justice do not appear to be anything spatial-temporal. I can also follow Lundstedt

[62] See the exposition of Hans Kelsen's conception of justice *supra* section 2. See also H. Kelsen: The Metamorphoses of the Idea of Justice, in P. Sayre (ed.): Interpretations of Modern Legal Philosophies, 1947, 390–418.

[63] See the exposition of Vilhelm Lundstedt's conception of justice *supra* section 2.

[64] Cf. L. Lavelle: De l'Etre, 2nd ed. 1947, 141: *„Dire que les illusions des nos rêves n'existent pas, c'est dire qu'elles n'existent que comme images, et qu'il ne faut pas les prendre pour des perceptions.“*

in his emphasis on the emotive and subjective nature of justice. His observations concerning justice may prove to be quite apt if properly interpreted. This interpretation requires, however, an effort because of his confusing and misleading expressions regarding values and justice (for example, „There is no justice", „The entire legal ideology goes up in smoke[65]").

The expression of the views such as those of Lundstedt, and perhaps even of Kelsen, tend to create the impression that their exponents have a strong bias against what is subjective and belongs to the emotive life, and consider it unworthy of the philosopher's and the legal theorist's attention. Views of this kind seem to me unfortunate. As has been rightly observed by Roscoe Pound, we should not surrender to the „give-it-up philosophy" which refuses to deal with the purely subjective[66]. The subjective may be a difficult but it is not an unworthy object of scholarly inquiries[67]. Even if this object is completely or largely alogical, irrational, it behooves us to subject it to our scrutiny. If it is beyond our powers to make the subjective lucid, we may nevertheless hope to render it less hazy, less mysterious. The fact that the subjective is not an entity that can be perceived through the senses is certainly not decisive for rejecting it as a legitimate matter of scholarly concern[68]. Much of our knowledge is gained only through reflection[69], among such knowledge being the laws of perception. Insofar as we find the subjective not amenable to rational apprehension, we have to define our proper attitude towards it[70].

The doubt as to whether an extension of the heueristic basis of my inquiry would not altogether destroy what seems common in all current

---

[65] Cf. A. Truyol: Doctrines Contemporaines du Droit des Gens, 1950, 54, Révue Générale du Droit Internationale Public, 377, who, criticising the doctrine of Lundstedt and other similar doctrines says: *„Au fond toutes ces doctrines sont construits a priori, elles ont un caractère dogmatique frappant"* (p. 381 ff.). For an *apologia* of legal science against Lundstedt's attacks see W. Fuchs: Die Zukunft der Rechtswissenschaft, 1933, 21–77. Cf. I. Tammelo: Drei rechtsphilosophische Aufsätze, 1948, 23–26.

[66] See R. Pound: Justice according to Law, 1951, 22 ff.

[67] Cf. A. Campbell Garnett: A Realistic Philosophy of Religion, 1942, 261, who observes that casting everything subjective, everything with which physical sciences cannot deal, is bad science and worse philosophy. „The psychological subject and all its contents are as much a part of the world order as summer and winter. There are no degrees of reality among concrete facts, and the value qualities of our inner experience are as much a fact as any other. Indeed they are the most important of all facts, for it is only in relation to them that other facts have importance."

[68] See Tammelo, op. cit. 23.

[69] Cf. C. J. Friedrich: Die Philosophie des Rechts in historischer Perspektive, 1955, 2, who emphasises that human experience *(die menschliche Erfahrung)* comprises also man's mental life *(das geistige und seelische Leben des Menschen)*.

[70] Cf. J. Stone: Legal Controls of International Conflict, 1954, 53 ff.

conceptions of justice[71] may be resolved by the following consideration: Granted that what is feared would prove to be the case, the heuristic basis for the notion of justice would still not be destroyed, because I can reject the material that frustrates my effort to find a sufficient number of common elements for a notion of justice. I could construe my notion of justice on the ground of the remaining material, employing what I rejected for construing another notion or other notions, for which I am, of course, obliged to give a name or names differing from „justice". This is a familiar method of scholarly procedure; it is a method for which the data of experience constitute only a base of departure but not a straightjacket. If I propose to obtain a notion of justice from some part of the material which my experience of *hic et nunc* existing notions of justice has provided me, I am free to do so. The fact that the notion thus obtained is not based on all potentially available data of experience does not render it incorrect. It may, of course, render it inept to serve the purposes for which it has been designed. A critic may very well find that the notions of justice with which I am operating are objectionable, and his views may very well prevail. But the prognosis of my notions of justice should not be a fetter for my inquiry either. It is my belief that a scholar does not seek to attain absolute intellectual values but works in the service of them both by his successes and failures, his insights and his errors[72]. It is essential that the data of experience constituting the base of his departure are not too limited nor the prognosis of his efforts too bad. I trust that neither is the case with the inquiry into the fundamentals of justice on which I am about to embark.

Having expressed the doubts which seemed to hinder entry to the inquiry into the fundamental principles of justice at all, I now ask, what do the above preliminary considerations of the notion of justice in language, legal thought, mythology, and philosophy yield for my venture to apprehend the principles on which the notion of justice is founded? It appears to me that, firstly, they yield some articulated thoughts required for delineation of an unstructured notion of justice, thoughts which are essential as points of departure for a rational penetration into it. Secondly, they bring out reserval incidental but illuminating matters surroundling the principles of justice such as the relations of affinity and tension in which justice stands to other entities of kindred nature.

For the purposes of my subsequent consideration of the fundamentals of justice, it is to be noted that it is consistent with the current notions of justice to use the word „justice" in an enveloping sense to mean anything that implies the notion „just". Thus „justice" is appropriate

[71] On the *prima vista* indications that „all the ideas of justice have something in common" see A. Brecht: Relative and Absolute Justice, in M. D. Forkosch: The Political Philosophy of Arnold Brecht, 1954, 21–48, at 34 ff.

[72] Cf. K. Jaspers: Philosophie, 2nd ed. 1948, 355: „He who wishes to be true, must have the courage to face the risk of error, and of putting himself in the wrong, must drive things to extremes and bring them to the knife's edge, so that they can be decided in truth and reality." (Transl. by Stone, op. cit. 321, n. 18).

as a general term for the whole theme of the present inquiry. For the sake of clarity it is, however, required to make distinctions which would articulate the loose usage of „justice" in order to be able to signify distinctly the following four notional entities: (1) „Justice" in the strict sense, which means a situation. (2) „Justice" in a metonymic sense, which means a character of something. For this notion the term „justness" is available. (3) „Justice" in a synecdochic sense, which means an attribute of something. For this notion the term „the just" can be used[73]. (4) „Justice" in the sense of a notion importing a value standard. For this notion the phrase „idea of justice" provides a convenient term.

This attempt to make the terminological distinctions raises the question, What is meant by „situation", „character", „attribute", and „idea"? The themes of this question constitute ontological problems. Reflecting on my preconceptual notion of justice, I find that there are philosophical problems of another nature requiring my attention. These problems are the cognition of justice, which is an epistemological problem; the formal structure of justice, which is a logical problem; and the relation of justice to values, which is an axiological problem.

Awareness of these problems relegates me to the first principles of philosophy. But what are these principles? How can I reach them? The great number of approaches to philosophy suggests that there may be alternative roads and that the inquirer may be free to choose his base of departure and his manner of approach. This freedom, however, does not make me very happy. What particular use shall I make of my freedom? I may start from where I am. But not today! Tomorrow when I shall resume my work on this essay, I may embark on my inquiries into the first principles of philosophy from where I then shall be.

Third Discourse

I wake up after a deep dreamless sleep and become aware that it is morning. I say to myself: „I wonder[74]." Immediately I notice that these words leave something open; they do not convey what I was wondering about. And now I wonder what did I wonder.

I am sure that I was wondering about something, but I cannot say definitely what this was. Perhaps I never knew; perhaps, if I knew, it immediately escaped my memory. That which I wondered about could have been the time of the day, could have been the event of my returning consciousness, but could also have been the question I left unanswered last night: Where to start in order to reach the fundamental principles

[73] „The just", like „the righteous", „the wicked", etc. is also used to designate persons who are just, righteous, wicked, etc. In the present essay this usage is not generally followed. The corresponding notions will be expressed by the phrases „just man", „unjust man", etc.

[74] Cf. K. Jaspers: Einführung in die Philosophie, 2nd ed. 1950, 26: and the translation of this work by R. Manheim: Way to Wisdom, 1951, 23: „The source of philosophy is to be sought in wonder, in doubt, in a sense of forsakenness" (literally: „ . . . in the experience of limit-situations").

of justice, the first principles of philosophy? Recalling this question, an answer offers itself to me which satisfies me: the statement „I wonder" can be my starting point. Reflecting on this simple statement and allowing my attention to fathom it and to rise above it, I hope to unfold my thoughts which would take me towards the desired end. In these unfolding thoughts I hope to find notions which permit me to relate justice to all other entities and to determine its place in the totality of everything of which I am able to be aware.

Trying to find a satisfying answer to the question, What did I wonder? I did not achieve any certainty about what the object of my wonder was. This lack of certainty may have been due to the fact that I was seeking an answer satisfying a particular curiosity of mine, a curiosity about what happened to me in one of the particular situations of my life. If I had been satisfied simply with „something" as an answer, I should have achieved certainty. How could I doubt that I wondered about something? The statement „I wonder about something" is completely evident to me as is the statement „There is something". I cannot conceive anything that would not be something, in other words, that would not be an entity. It is evident to me that everything is something[75], is an entity.

Accepting that everything is something, I have to accept also that every element of the statement „I wonder" is an entity: thus „I" is an entity, „wonder" is an entity, and even the whole statement containing the two elements is an entity. The proposition „Everything is something" imports that there is a fundamental notion „something" or „entity" of unrestricted universality, the scope of which must comprise also justice.

The same character of universality does not appear to belong to „I". „I" is a singularity, a particular entity, an entity that wonders, doubts, reflects, is certain about, and performs other acts of the same kind here and now. Being an event that occurs here and now, „I" is a unique entity; it is an entity whose apprehension is intimate to me and is, as I believe, intimate to all other entities which are capable of experiencing wonder and of reflecting on it. These other entities and myself I denote by a common notion, using for it the name „Ego". The performance of various acts which constitutes an ego I propose to call „cogitation". When an ego wonders, reflects, or doubts: whenit enjoys or suffers, thinks, feels, or wills — it cogitates[76]. Since cogitation is what constitutes an ego, the statement *„Cogito ergo sum sive existo"*[77] is completely evident to me[78].

---

[75] On the problem of „something", especially in relation to the categories „existence" and „subsistence" see M. White: Toward Reunion in Philosophy, 1956, 63 ff.

[76] Cf. Descartes: Meditationes de Prima Philosophia (ed. by C. Guttler, 1901), 92.

[77] In the Cartesian dictum, *„cogito"* can be regarded as the central theme of epistemology, *„ergo"* the central theme of logic, and *„sum"* the central theme of the philosophy of human life.

[78] For a critical analysis of the Cartesian formula *„cogito ergo sum sive existo"* see J. Anderson, The Cogito of Descartes, 1936, 14, Australasian Journal of Psychology and Philosophy, 48—68.

Havin reflected on my statement: „I wonder", which referred to a state *(status)* of my mind *(mens)*, I notice that the unfolding of my thoughts has occurred in a great variety of notions. Thinking of this variety, I wonder whether all these notions, apart from being entities and referring to entities, have something else in common. I apprehend that there *are* entities, that I *am* a wondering ego, that something *is* certain, and that whenever there is *cogito*, there is *sum*. „Are", „am", „is", and other words of the same kind appear all to name different forms of a basic circumstance, which I propose to call „Being". „Being" as a notion appears to have the same unrestricted universality as the notion „Entity[79]". Nevertheless Being and Entity do not appear to be identical entities. I apprehend them as two distinct fundamental circumstances which I posit through different modes of referring. „Entity" I posit through predicative referring, whereas „Being" I posit through copulative referring.

The reflection which I started when I wondered about my wonder has led me into a train of thought which I hope will bring me some clarity about the fundamentals of justice. Despite this hope I have perceived an undercurrent of doubt from the very outset of my reflection, a doubt as to whether I was thinking on a right plane along correct lines towards a promising end. To proceed in my effort to apprehend the fundamentals of justice seems forbidden to me before I have voiced these doubts, discussed them, and at least partially overcome them.

When I said to myself: „I wonder", and when I started my reflection on this statement, I thought I was thinking of something very simple. This simplicity I abandoned in the further course of my reflection. Was I not assuming an artificial attitude by trying to be simple? Is there any merit in a simple starting point of philosophical reflection at all?

This doubt I can dispel by the following consideration: I have never intended to commit myself unqualifiedly to an intellectual naïveté by trying to be simple. In intellectual naïveté I cannot see any other merit than that of providing provisional cognitive situations which do not lure the mind astray with the ramifications of their implications, and which do not confuse it with their ambiguity. Even for a mind trained in abstruse thinking it may be sometimes good to begin reflection from simple situations, especially when in the process of thinking certain issues have become blurred. The problem of the fundamentals of justice, like all problems of fundamental principles, is abstruse, and I cannot reasonably hope to achieve any clarity about it unless I engage all the faculties of my mind which have a bearing on my problem. During the course of my studies I have acquired certain ways, tools, and products of thinking which permit my thoughts to evolve in a discursive manner, but which also enable me to gain appropriate intuitions about the matters to be apprehended. All this I have acquired in a community of work with others, from whom I have learnt, with whom I have exchanged ideas,

---

[79] On the notion of entity cf. S. Alexander: Space, Time, and Deity, 3rd impr. 1950, vol. I, p. 176.

and to whom I have communicated my thoughts. I can communicate with those who have themselves thought along lines similar to mine without any need to abandon my own intellectual background. The quest of the fundamentals of a problem requires not only a naïve mind but also a mind that has lost its intellectual innocence through learning, a mind to whom the homecoming to a naïveté must always be something provisional. Keen intuitions are provided not only by a naïve mind but also by a learned mind as well. Some essential intuitions for the apprehension of the fundamentals of a problem like justice appear to be attainable only by learned minds. And for a learned mind the assuming of the attitude of naïveté itself seems to require some degree of sophistication.

The other doubt which disturbs me about my reflection on the statement „I wonder" is the truth of the assertions I made in the course of the unfolding of my thoughts. The question as to whether these assertions are true finds an answer if I consider that they all have been made in terms „It appears to me[80]", even though this phrase has not, in order to avoid monotony, always been used. Thus these assertions are, with regard to their truth, equivalent to such statements as „I see a tree before me", which holds irrespective of whether there is a tree to be seen or not. Doubt about their truth can arise only in two ways: first, if I may have been dishonest and stated something which really was not the case; second, if at the time when I made the assertion, I had fallen into error about what appeared to me when it originally appeared. The first doubt I can conquer with my faith in my own scholarly integrity, the second one by a hope for good luck in avoiding the demon of error[81].

But in connection with the doubt about the truth of my assertions a much graver doubt arises. My assertions were not intended to be solely my own private affair. I have uttered them in order to communicate them to others. They were intended to be intersubjective. How can I warrant their truth to others? It is not enough that others accept my scholarly integrity and my belief in my good luck in avoiding errors in the steps of my reasoning. My assertions, to be of real value, must somehow transcend the „It appears to me" and assume the status of „It appears to us", or simply „It appears". This transcending is conceivable on the assumption that there is a basic commonness of mind in *homo sapiens,* which permits that the same intuitions can be achieved by everyone if the addresser and the addressee seek to reach each other's intellectual level. Even for this search there are obstacles, barriers of human communication, but *homo sapiens* being also *homo faber* and *homo ludens* has faculties to overcome them through properly directed effort. Assertions such as those in the present discourse I conceive as invitations to others to think along

[80] On the philosophical meaning of the word „appears" see S. E. Toulmin: The Place of Reason in Ethics, 1950, 126 ff. On appearing, especially in relation to sense-data, see R. M. Chisholm: The Theory of Appearing, in M. Black (ed.): Philosophical Analysis, 1950, 102–119.

[81] Cf. L. Wittgenstein: Philosophical Investigations (transl. G. E. M. Anscombe, 1953), 49, § 123: „A philosophical problem has the form: ‚I do not know my way about'."

the same lines as my own; they are calls for making efforts to overcome communication barriers, and attempts to transcend the „It appears to me“ towards „It appears to us“ through joined efforts to communicate, by which efforts reason has a chance to assert itself, a chance that in isolated thoughts and isolated works it never can have.

In this connection a still graver doubt comes to my awareness. Should not the „It appears“ be transcended altogether as something provisional. Are not what we are actually striving after certain universal truths and not truths which exist for private minds capable of entering into unobstacled human communication? For this doubt I cannot find any other remedy than to renounce the claim to have pronounced universally valid truths in the present discourse. I consider my reflection here like a groping[82] for a key which I hope would unlock a door from the enclosure of my private mind to a common terrain from where vistas of the universe can be seen by and shown to everyone. There may be many keys, many doors, and many places to which these doors lead serving the same end. It may, however, also be that the key I have sought opens the door to a *mundus fabulosus* revealing only illusions and no „realities“. This may be so, but I still feel I have to go on with my search. If I have an untimely apprehension about the universality of the truth of my assertions, I shall be spellbound even in my groping for the key[83].

The attempt to clear away the above doubts by reflection on my reflection makes me aware that my reasoning has moved in circles. Thus I could not help thinking of „Entity“ and „Being“ otherwise than in notions which were entities or had being themselves. I have thought that perhaps I should have remained silent — to follow a councel of Ludwig Wittgenstein[84] — every time when I entered into a *circulus vitiosus*. Yet it seems to me that silence in these cases would not have been the proper attitude. I was not trying to prove anything or to deduce anything. I was only engaged in search for certain basic intuitions, was trying to point them out, to focus my own and my reader's mind to them. Thus the rules of definition and demonstration could not bind me. This indicating and focusing could very well take place by showing the context in which the entity sought occured, in pointing to the configuration of entities where it occured.

My mind being, for the time being, at quiet concerning the viscious circle in which my reflection seemed to be moving, the following doubt still remains. „Being“ and „Entity“ seem to have no opposites. Not-being must also have being in view of the unrestricted universality of

---

[82] Cf. C. I. Lewis: An Analysis of Knowledge and Valuation, 1946, 357 ff. on „mnemic preservation of past experience“ and on the need to limit the Cartesian doubt in relation to it. On the validity of memory in general see ibid. ch. xi.

[83] I find a certain reassurance in the thought that I am treading a path not untrodden by others, and I have companions even in my failure and frustration.

[84] See L. Wittgenstein: Tractatus Logico-Philosophicus, 3rd impr. 1947, 189: „Whereof one cannot speak, thereof one must be silent.“

Being[85], and Nothing must also be something, must be an entity[86]. Thus both notions, comprising also their contradictions must resolve into nothingness. But if this is so, the notion „nothingness" becomes a problem, and its solution would obviously meet no smaller difficulties than the problem of „Being" and „Entity". A way out of the present dilemma seems to be that the ultimate ontological notions such as „Being" and „Entity" are outside the scope of the requirements concerning the formation of ordinary concepts and as such may be governed by the principle of *coincidentia oppositorum*. Such notions are limit-notions not unlike the notions of infinity and zero in mathematics[87]. Just as mathematical limit-notions they require caution in their handling to avoid mistakes which may occur confusing them with ordinary notions.

Having doubted about the various aspects of my reflection, a doubt about my doubting itself confronts me. I doubt whether my doubts have been comprehensive enough and radical enough. My attention being directed to this matter, I become aware of a large inarticulate doubt, an aggregate of doubts which I cannot properly voice. And there is even the doubt whether the voiced doubts have been appropriate and appropriately voiced. This encloses me in a vicious circle of doubt, the dwelling in

---

[85] See L. Lavelle: La Présence Totale, 1934, 48; id.: De l'Etre, 2nd ed. 1947, 12, 53.

[86] Cf. Lewis, op. cit. 88, who characterises the notions „Being" and „Entity" as having zero intension and universal comprehension. Cf. also P. Tillich: Love, Power, and Justice, 1954, 38: „Non-being is the negation of being within being itself." And cf. the notion of Non-being in Vedic thought, about which Professor Jaan Puhvel has kindly supplied the following learned note:

„Regarding the ontological status of Non-being, it is interesting to note that the problem is treated at least half a millennium before the earliest Ionian philosophers in the most remarkable cosmogonic hymn of the Rig-Veda (X. 129). By general Vedic philosophical opinion Being arose from Non-being, but this poem takes the position that in the beginning neither existed, and they came about only through the creation which also brought forth the gods:

X. 129. 1: *násad āsīn nó sád āsīt tadā́nīm*
,Non-being was not, nor was Being then'

ibid. 2: *ná mrtyúr āsīd amŕ̥tam ná tárhi*
,death was not, nor deathlessness then'

ibid. 4: *sató bándhum ásati nír avindan hr̥dí pratī́ṣyā kaváyo manīṣā́*
,the seers, searching in the heart with wisdom, found a relative of Being in Non-being'.

That is, they found the inherent close relationship and interdependence of both. By implication, the ontological equality of Being and Non-being is affirmed. The ultimate pre-creational origin of the world remains obscure to the poet." Cf. for a commentary, translation, and further references K. F. Geldner: Der Rig-Veda, 1951, vol. III, 359–361.

[87] On the philosophical problems of infinity and zero see B. Russell: Introduction to Mathematical Philosophy, 8th impr. 1953, 1–28, 63–96; 131–143.

which is uncomfortable to me even if I think: *cum dubio sum*. But somehow I must reconcile myself to being in doubt as I have to see some purpose in my dwelling and wayfaring in the world. I must only beware that being in doubt would not paralyse my efforts to think and to search. I must rather find a dynamic force, something that is constructive, for my inquiries in my inclination to doubting[88]. If required, I can reduce the intensity of my doubting in any given case by doubting the value of my doubting itself, but I should not hesitate to voice again my doubts at any time when I become aware of them and when there seems to be a necessity to discuss them.

II. Ontological Considerations

5. On the Categories of Being and of Entity

An ontological inquiry into justice involves the task of considering the being of justice and justice as an entity. To acquire the ontological grounding for the clarification of justice, it is necessary to traverse the spheres of both Being and Entity in order to become acquainted with these ultimate ontological posits at their principal points. These points are ontological categories[89].

A prevelant feature of these categories is that any of them is a correlative of another[90], together with which it is constituted and without which it is inconceivable. Another prevalent feature of them is their pervasiveness: a category or its correlative reaches all Being and is relevant for any entity[91]. Like the notions of Being and Entity, the notions of their categories are ontological limit-notions, and as such have features and functions distinct from ordinary notions. To apprehend the specific status of categories, it is perhaps appropriate to regard them as specific values: as entities which the inquirer considers that they ought to be for the purpose of apprehending the fundamental principles of what is there. Thus the sought concepts of categories would not only be *con-cepta* of propositions (in terms of which ordinary concepts can be analysed) but also *con-cepta* of non-propositional statements[92]. If this viewpoint is taken, the ontological categories provide not only themes of assertions[93] but also themes of questions and suppositions, and perhaps even themes of desires which the inquiring mind

[88] For the classical statement of skepticism as a principle of inquiry see Hume: An Inquiry concerning Human Understanding, s. xii („Of the Academical or Sceptical Philosophy").

[89] On the problem of categories see generally, A. Trendelenburg: Geschichte der Kategorienlehre, 1846; E. von Hartmann: Kategorienlehre, 1923, in 3 volumes; S. Alexander: Space, Time, and Deity, 3rd impr. 1950, vol. I, bk. ii; E. Husserl: Formale und transzendentale Logik, 1929; N. Hartmann: Der Aufbau der realen Welt, 2nd ed. 1949.

[90] See Hartmann: Aufbau, 265–352.

[91] Cf. Alexander, op. cit. I, pp. 201, 343.

[92] For this classification of statements see *infra* s. 9.

[93] On the problem of the defining of the ontological notions see Alexander, op. cit. I, p. viii.

experiences in relation to the ultimate foundation of everything that confronts it. When ontological categories are tried to be clarified by „pointing to" them by questions (as this will be attempted below)[94], the problem arises, What is meant by saying that something is a theme of a question? An answer to this can be given only by referring to certain basic but familiar experiences of every inquiring mind. A question is an act by which something is posed as a problem, or by which something is wondered about. The problem posed, the „about"[95] of the wondering, is the *thema* of the *thesis* given in the form of a question.

The questions for which the ontological categories provide themes appear to be perennial questions; they constantly refer to something encompassing, to the Boundless, to the *ἄπειρον*. Delineating the inquirer's approaches towards his cognitive horizon, the notions of ontological categories are periechontological notions withal[96]. Because of non-propositional features and functions of these notions and the horizonal character of ontological inquiries, truth and falsity may be considered as something secondary for ontological findings. Ontological problems, therefore, can be approached by *intentio recta*[97], in which the inquirer simply takes notice of what is encountered by his intellect — what simply appears to it[98]. A restraint is imposed on him not so much by the danger of falling into error as by the consideration of relevance. An ontological statement is irrelevant if it does not support in any way the pursuits for which it is used as an instrument; as such it may be pointless, absurd, but not objectionable on the grounds of falsity[99].

---

[94] These questions will be asked in as abstract and general terms as possible in order to avoid disturbing and distracting intuitions which may be attached to notions of more concrete and particular nature, that also could be used to ask these questions. This manner of asking does not allow the expressions of the questions to be always quite idiomatic, and it must have some adverse effect upon the intellegibility of the questions. I have tried to make the sense of the questions more intelligible by illustrating them by examples. As regards the non-idiomatic character of their expression, all I can say is that ordinary language has not been designed for ontological purposes. I presume that there is no natural language in the world which would not suffer some violence by being made a vehicle of ontological discussions.

[95] On the problem of the meaning of „about" see M. White: Toward Reunion in Philosophy, 1956, 31 ff.

[96] Cf. K. Jaspers: Von der Wahrheit, 1947, 47—222; cf. also Alexander, op. cit. I, p. 183.

[97] On *intentio recta* see N. Hartmann: Zur Grundlegung der Ontologie, 3rd ed. 1948, 49—51. Cf. J. Llambías de Azevedo: The Eidetics and the Aporetics of the Law, in vol. III of 20th Century Legal Philosophy Series (transl. by G. Ireland, 1948), 403—458, at 403—411; Alexander, op. cit. I, p. 11; B. Russell: An Outline of Philosophy, 1927, 134.

[98] Cf. P. Tillich: Love, Power, and Justice, 1954, 23: „Ontology is descriptive, not speculative. It analyses the encountered reality, trying to find the structural elements which enable a being to participate in being."

[99] On the verification of ontological propositions see op. cit. 24.

In the sphere of Being the following categorial correlatives can be encountered through ontological *intentio recta:* Essence and Sistence, the two principal aspects of Being; Becoming and Enduring, the two principal states of Being; Possibility and Actuality, the two principal modes of Being; and Ideality and Reality, the two principal realms of Being.

Essence is the theme of the question: What is the entity E?, whereas Sistence is the theme of the question: Is the entity E there[100]? For example, the determination of the essence (or „thus-being") of a book involves the determination of everything by which it is constituted as an entity distinct from other entities, whereas the ascertainment of the sistence (or „there-being") of a book involves the taking of notice that it is. Both „essence" and „sistence" are notions of such unrestricted universality that it is impossible to conceive something without an essence or something without sistence[101]. „Not-sisting" can mean only not-being-there-as-such[102]. This latter meaning falls under the ontological notion „Absence"[103], the correlative of which is „Presence". „Not-having-essence" can mean only not having a particular essence. The category „Sistence" has two sub-categories: Subsistence and Existence. An entity has subsistence if something else is *of* this entity as of an entity that founds, conditions, and underlies. An entity has existence if it is of something else as founded, conditioned, derived. Subsistence and Existence are correlatives, therefore whenever there is a subsisting X there is an existing Y, which exists in relation to the X; and whenever there is an existing Y, there is a subsisting X, which subsists in relation to this Y. A subsisting entity can be an existing entity in relation to a third entity. Thus X subsisting in relation to Y may exist in relation to Z, which subsists in relation to X (and, of course, also in relation to Y). There appears to be only one entity which only subsists but does not exist: the totality of everything or the All (the Absolute).

Possibility is the theme of the question, Can the entity E be there as it is assumed to be there? Actuality is the theme of the question, is the entity E there as it is assumed to be there? What is actual is also possible, and what is impossible can never be actual. Hence actuality presupposes possibility[104], but not *vice versa.* Actuality has two sub-

---

[100] Cf. Nicolai Hartmann's distinction of *Sosein* and *Dasein* in his *Grundlegung,* 88—149. Cf. also K. Engisch: Logische Studien zur Gesetzesanwendung, 1943, 40 ff.

[101] Cf. A. Boyce-Gibson: The Philosophy of Descartes, 1943, 323.

[102] Cf. W. Brock's account of *Sein und Zeit* in M. Heidegger: Existence and Being (transl. by W. Brock, 1949), 83.

[103] Cf. L. Lavelle: De l'Etre, 2nd ed. 1947, 40 ff.

[104] Cf. E. Husserl: Ideas: General Introduction to Pure Phenomenology (transl. by W. R. Boyce Gibson, 1931), 232: „The old ontological doctrine, *that the knowledge of „possibilities" must precede that of actualities* . . . is . . . in so far as it is rightly understood and properly utilised, a really great truth." On the problem of the modes of Being see generally N. Hartmann: Möglichkeit und Wirklichkeit, 2nd ed. 1949, esp. pp. 45—60. On the intermodal laws see ibid. 60—102.

ordinate modes: necessity and contingency. Something that *is* actual may be such that it *must be* actual, in which case it is necessary. Otherwise it is contingent. The subordinate modes of possibility are potentiality, which is an actualisable but not yet actualised possibility, and mere possibility, which is a conceivable but not actualisable possibility.

Becoming is the theme of the question, What is the subsistence of the circumstance that the entity E which was or is x is or will be non-x? Enduring is the theme of the question, What is the subsistence of the circumstance that the entity E which was or is x is or will be x? For example, Becoming is involved where a thing is in motion, but also where emotions change or thoughts evolve. There appears to be, however, no universal flux (Herakleitean *πάντα ῥεῖ*) since the flux itself is inconceivable if there is nothing in it or about it to endure. If there is nothing else in the Universe to endure, its becoming at least endures.

Reality or Ontic Being is the theme of the question, What is the subsistence of the becoming of the entity E? The becoming of entities can occur either in time only or in space and time[105]. In the former case their being is noëtic[106], in the latter case their being is hyletic. Hyletic being consists of physical-material being, organic being, and psychical being. These domains of Reality appear to have a „stratified structure" in the sense that the first is a condition of the second, and the second is the condition of the third. Considering that noëtic being appears to require psychical being, and together with it the entire hyletic being, as its condition, it may be said that the whole of Ontic Being has a stratified structure[107]. Ideality or Eidetic Being[108] is the theme of the question, What is the subsistence of the enduring of the entity E? In the realm of Eidetic Being the following domains can be distinguished: Inherent Being, Adherent Being, and Extraherent Being. An entity has inherent being if it is a constituent of another entity. An entity has adherent being if it is attributable or attributed to another entity without belonging to this entity as its constituent. An entity has extraherent being if it is neither inherent in or adherent to another entity. For example, the logical structure of a statement is inherent in a statement whose logical structure it is; values such as the beautiful, the right, and the good are adherent to the entities to which they are attributed; and the noumenal entities such as Eternity and the Absolute are extraherent in relation to phenomenal entities.

---

[105] Cf. S. Alexander: Space, Time, and Deity, 3rd impr. 1950, vol. II, p. 41: „... Space-Time is the matrix of all empirical existence."

[106] On the reality of noëtic being (of „ideas") see Alexander, op. cit. II, p. 67 ff.

[107] On the structure of Ontic Being see Hartmann: Aufbau, 171–218. See also Alexander: op. cit. II, p. 67 ff.

[108] In the subsequent inquiries I shall use „eidetic being" and „ontic being" in preference to „ideality" and „reality" because of the widely ambiguous use of the latter terms.

In the sphere of Entity[109] the following categorial correlatives can be encountered through ontological *intentio recta:* Principle and Concretum, Relation and Relatum, Unity and Plurality, Subject and Object. Principle is the theme of the question, What is the subsisting entity E as an actuality? Concretum is the theme of the question, What is an existing entity E as an actuality? For example, the whole event of the fall of a body is a concretum, whereas the laws of physics determining this event are principles. Relation is the theme of the question, What is the entity that is there as a togetherness of other entities? Relatum is the theme of the question, What is the entity that is there as an entity being together with another entity? For example, a legal obligation is a relation, whereas the right which the one party has and the duty which the other party has are the relata of this relation. Unity is the theme of the question, What is the entity that is there as being one? Plurality is the theme of the question, What is the entity that is there as being many? For example, an electron is a unity, but a molecule is a plurality. There are, of course also unities which are pluralities, for instance, a class, a town, and a molecule. Subject is the theme of the question, What is the entity that is there as an entity to which another entity is something? Object is the theme of the question[110], What is an entity that is there as an entity which is something to another entity[111]? For example, a person who makes intellectual efforts to solve a problem, is a thinking subject, whereas the problem to be solved is an object of these efforts; in the process of growth of a plant the growing plant is a subject of this process, whereas any stage of the development of the plant to which the growth leads is an object of this process.

The ontological notions can be combined with each other in various ways to form other ontological notions. In view of the pervasiveness and interpenetration of ontological categories[112], the latter may be those which appear to the ontological *intentio recta* of an inquirer first, who then may employ them for apprehending the ontological categories which were above pointed to. Combination of the notions of the above categories makes it possible to seek the apprehension of other categories or subcategories by following propositions: The subsisting entity is Substance[113]. The unity of plurality is Totality. The totality of everything

[109] On the problem of the notion „Entity“ see generally A. N. Prior: Entities, 1954, 32, Australasian Journal of Philosophy, 159—168. Note Prior's thesis that there are abstract entities (p. 154).

[110] Cf. G. Del Vecchio: Ethics, Law, and the State, 1935, 46, International Journal of Ethics, 34, at 34: „Subject and object are not ‚thing‘ or matter, but transcendental criteria, which means necessary *(a priori)* points of view.“

[111] It may be said that an object is an entity in one of the particular functions of Entity. Entity evidently embraces also Subject, a subject being an entity in another specific function of Entity. Thus there are subjects and objects of cognition, of valuation; grammatical subjects and objects, legal subjects and objects, etc. They all are entities.

[112] See Hartmann: Aufbau, 447—458.

[113] On the problem of Substance see M. Lazerowitz: Substratum, in M. Black (ed.): Philosophical Analysis, 1950, 176—194.

is the All. A relatum which does not consist of any relations is Substratum. An entity which has inherent being is Character: An entity which has adherent being is Attribute[114]. The unity of characters or of a character is Structure. A component part of a structure is Element. An entity which is the principle of becoming of something is Act. An entity which has become a concretum is Fact. A becoming entity is Event[115]. An entity which is inherent or adherent to another entity is Quality. A state of being is Circumstance.

The above ontological sketch has not been intended as a closed table of the categories. Questions can be asked in different ways, suppositions and desires can be put forward in different manners. Thus various systems of categories can be construed, and many of these systems may be appropriate matrices for inquiries into the fundamental principles of a particular problem. A system serving as such matrix may very well be an open set of notions allowing additions, revision and refinements. The above attempts to clarify the categories could not amount to anything more than to efforts towards an ostensive defining of the categories. Such definitions, by their very nature, appear to constitute an open procedure. Thus the occurrence of the notions of categories in the subsequent contexts of the present inquiry is, to some extent, a continuation of the procedure of their defining by ostension.

6. The Ontological Aspect of Justice

The ontological notions specified in the previous section are instruments for analysing justice on the basis of the unstructured notions obtained of justice in the preliminary considerations of the present inquiry. They are also means for inordinating the *analysata* in a system of thought. In the Second Discourse, which completed the preliminary considerations, „justice" was distinguished in four different senses: „justice" in the strict sense, signifying a situation; „justness", signifying a character; „the just", signifying an attribute; and „the idea of justice", signifying a notion.

What is designated by „justice" in the senses thus distinguished can now be analysed by recourse to the categories of Being as follows: Justice, justness, the just, and the idea of justice all have sistence as well as essence considering that these ontological categories are of unrestricted universality. Hence, under the present ontological scheme Lundstedt's contention: „There is no justice" cannot assert that justice has no sistence but only that justice is absent in a particular place, time, or mode. Any proposition asserting that justice has no essence would likewise be untenable under the present ontological scheme. The absence of the essence of justice, which such propositions may attemp to assert, can ontologically succeed only in asserting that justice lacks

[114] Cf. S. E. Toulmin: The Place of Reason in Ethics, 1950, 10 ff. Alexander, op. cit. II, pp. 246, 302.

[115] On the notion of event see A. N. Whitehead: Science and the Modern World, 12th impr. 1953, 91, 149 ff.

a certain kind of essence. The sistence of justice, justness, the just, and the idea of justice can be either subsistence or existence, depending on whether they are founding or founded entities for other entities in relation to which they are considered.

Justice, justness, the just, and the idea of justice all appear to exist[116] at least as possibilities. They are there as possibilities because they appear to be free from self-contradiction; the distinctions made in Second Discourse of „justice“ in its four specific senses should have constituted what each particular sense of the word refers to as a conceivable entity. The actuality of what is designated by „justice“ appears to have the following conditions: Justice is actual if a situation is deemed to have justness. Justness is actual if the just is attributed to an entity which conforms[117] to the attribute „just“. If an entity conforms to the attribute „just“ but the character „justness“ has not been predicated by anyone of this entity, then justness is only a potentiality. The just is actual if the attribute „just“ is experienced as a distinct entity by a concrete intellect. The idea of justice is actual if justice as an actuality or as a possibility is apprehended by a concrete intellect. „A mere idea of justice“ is no less an actuality than an idea of justice referring to an entity which is actual; for example, in cases of revolutionary ideas of justice, an idea of justice which is still a mere idea may be of terrific actuality in the conditions of a revolution. It should be noted that the conformity of an entity to an attribute does not appear to be identical with the character corresponding to this attribute. Thus the conformity to the attribute „just“ does not appear to be identical with justness[118]. The conformity to an attribute is a potentiality of an entity which potentiality founds the attributability of an attribute to the entity, in other words, it is not a character of an entity but a predicability of a character of an entity[119]. Hence it may be said that a stone, a tree, or an animal does not have conformity to the just. However, a person, a behaviour of a person, or a social situation has such conformity. Justness of a person is a virtue (of this person)[120]. Justice which is actual is a realised idea of justice. „Realisation of justice“ means that the potential social situation to which an idea of justice refers is becoming or has become an actual social situation.

Analysing justice, justness, the just, and the idea of justice as actualities by recourse to the categories of the states of Being and of realms of Being, the following circumstances are encountered by the

---

116 Cf. E. W. Hall: What Is Value? 1952, 225: „There is value . . .“

117 On the concept of value-conformity cf. A. Meinong: Psychologisch-ethische Untersuchungen zur Werttheorie, 1894, 25. Cf. also S. Alexander: Space, Time, and Deity, 3rd impr. 1950, vol. I, p. 188, vol. II, p. 241 ff.

118 Cf. J. Anderson: Determinism in Ethics, 1928, 6, Australasian Journal of Psychology and Philosophy, 241, at 243, who conceives value as „conformity to a standard“.

119 Cf. C. I. Lewis: An Analysis of Knowledge and Valuation, 1946, ch. xviii, esp. pp. 521 and 524.

120 Cf. E. Wolf: Das Problem der Naturrechtslehre, 1955, 90.

ontological *intentio recta*. As actualities, justice and the idea of justice appear to be events, that is, entities subject to becoming; they therefore have ontic being. Justness and the just appear not to be events; they have eidetic being. Since „justice" in the strict sense designates a social situation[121], and a social situation always exists not only in a certain time but also in a certain place, justice as an actuality belongs to the domain of hyletic being. Since „the idea of justice" designates a notion, and notions are characterised only by temporality, the idea of justice belongs to the domain of noëtic being. The noëtic being of the idea of justice does not depend on whether this idea refers to justice as an actuality or justice as a possibility. Even an idea of a mere possibility is a notion existing in a certain time, and as such it has noëtic being. The eidetic being of justness is inherence, whereas the eidetic being of the just is adherence. As eidetic entities, justness and the just can be also characterised as being not subject to becoming; the state of being peculiar to them is enduring. In contrast to justness and the just, justice and the idea of justice are subject to becoming. As events, justice existing in the place P at the moment M may become different in some or in many of its features at the moment M_1 and an idea of justice existing at the moment N may become changed at the moment N_1. As unactualised or unactualisable possibilities, justice, justness, the just, and the idea of justice have eidetic being. This is evident in respect of justness and the just, which are eidetic entities even as actualities. But this appears to be the case also in respect of justice and the idea of justice if it is considered that even though justice and the idea of justice as possibilities are apprehended as inordinated in a space-time matrix, the space-time in question must be a possible space-time and as such it would not allow a possible justice or a possible idea of justice to be ontic entities. It may be stated as an ontological law that the possibilities of ontic entities have eidetic being.

Analysing justice, justness, the just, and the idea of justice by recourse to the categories of Entity, the following circumstances are encountered by the ontological *intentio recta:* They all are principles where they are considered as entities founding the existence of other entities. Thus they may be principles of a legal or moral order. Justice, and the idea of justice are concreta where they are considered to be entities existing in a determined time or space-time. The just is a concretum where it is attributed by a mind to an entity. Justness is a concretum where it is predicated by a mind of an entity. It can also be said that justice, justness, the just, and the idea of justice are concreta in all cases when they are actual.

Where justice, justness, the just, and the idea of justice are apprehended in relation to each other or in relation to other entities, they occur as relata. Justice and the idea of justice appear to have a

---

[121] On the concept of situation see Alexander, op. cit. I, p. 240; P. Weiss: The Real Art Object, 1956, 16, Philosophy and Phenomenological Research, 341, at 347.

complex structure; they are relations. In contrast to them, justness and the just appear to be simple (substratal) entities. Justice, justness, the just, and the idea of justice are each qualities: justice is the quality of the society in which a situation deemed to have justness eventuates, the idea of justice is a quality of the mind in which this idea exists as a notion, justness as a character is an inherent quality of the entity deemed to have justness, and the just as an attribute is an adherent quality for the entity to which it is attributed. It may be noted that justness is not an inherent quality of the entity E(a) to which the just is attributed but an inherent quality of the entity E(p) of which justness is predicated. E(p) is an entity constituted by the attribution of the just to E(a). The attribution makes the object of attribution (that is E[a]) appear in a particular „light" or „mood"; it does not produce any change in this object itself[122]. The entity that may be called „appearance-of-an-entity-in-a-particular-mood" (that is E[p]), however, is an entity different from the object of attribution (that is E [a]), and the quality attributed to the latter is for the former an inherent quality, that is, a character[123].

Justice, justness, the just, and the idea of justice can be objects in various ways. For example, the just as an attribute can be an object of philosophical inquiry, justness can be an object of political concern, justice can be an object of thought of those who appear as litigants before a court, and the idea of justice can be an object of interest in cultural history. All these four entities can also be subjects. For example, justice can be a subject of change when social conditions evolve, the idea of justice can be subject to evolution in a given mind or in a given cultural situation. The just and justness can eventuate as logical subjects of a proposition.

What has been said above may suffice for the apprehension of the main ontological features of justice, justness, the just and the idea of justice. A fuller use of the categorial matrix presented in the previous section will be made in the subsequent course of this inquiry, in which an attempt will be made to clarify the epistemological, logical, and axiological aspects of justice.

III. Epistemological Considerations

7. On Cognition, Knowledge, and Truth

To be aware of justice and to be able to act in regard to justice, it appears to be possible to dispense with knowing what this awareness and this acting involve. To a certain extent man can orient in the world and achieve his practical purposes even without being clear on the cognitive events and elements involved in the acquaintance with the

[122] Cf. F. K. Beutel: Experimental Jurisprudence, 1957, 37–44.

[123] On the notions of attribution (ascription) and predication see Lewis, op. cit. 388 ff.

entities that confront him[124]. Such apprehension does not suffice for the purposes of the present inquiry. The principles of cognition, knowledge, and truth belong to the fundamentals of justice. Without clarifying them no requisite clarity can be expected about the central theme of this essay.

Knowledge is a state of being arising through the process of cognition. It can be characterised as a cognitive awareness of something. Thus one may know that it is five o'clock, that it is warm, that twice two is four, and that virtue is good whereas vice is bad. The specific character of knowledge is that it is verified and founded. An awareness which arises through the process of cognition can also be unverified and unfounded, can be a mere belief. Knowledge and mere belief are kinds of belief. A belief can be regarded as true or false, verified or unverified, even though final, absolute verification can never be assumed. A belief being true means that reasons exist which substantiate it, although these reasons may not be given or known. A belief being verified means that reasons are actually given for substantiating it, although they may not be sufficient to substantiate it[125].

Ontologically, cognition and its end product knowledge belong to noëtic being[126], whereas truth belongs to eidetic being. It may be said that Being is more fundamental than Knowing, or to use a metaphorical phrase: Knowledge is embedded in Being. The philosophical discipline which inquires into cognition, knowledge, and truth is epistemology (or theory of knowledge). The central theme of epistemology is the epistemological relation, the relata of which are the epistemological subject (or the intellect) and the epistemological object. In its dynamic aspect the epistemological relation is the cognitive relation, a relation in which the cogniser is confronted with the cognised. In its static aspect the epistemological relation is the relation of belief or the relation of knowledge in which the believer or the knower is confronted with the believed or the known[127]. The epistemological relation is a correlation: an intellect without something believed, cognised or known — and a belief, cognition, or knowledge without an intellect — are inconceivable.

One of the principal tasks of epistemology is to reflect upon how the epistemological object is given to the intellect[128]. In this reflection the subject seems to be transcended, that is, this reflection „extends"

---

[124] Cf. B. Russell: Our Knowledge of the External World, 1914, 21. On the problem of knowledge in general see C. I. Lewis: An Analysis of Knowledge and Valuation, 1946; N. Hartmann: Grundzüge einer Metaphysik der Erkenntnis, 4thed. 1949; B. Russell: Human Knowledge, Its Scope and Limits, 1948.

[125] Cf. Lewis, op. cit. ch. ix, esp. p. 254 ff.

[126] See N. Hartmann: Der Aufbau der realen Welt, 2nd ed. 1949, ch. 18, esp. p. 171 ff.

[127] On the epistemological relation see J. Anderson: The Knower and the Known, 1926/27, 27, Proceedings of the Aristotelian Society, 61, esp. p. 62 ff.

[128] Since epistemology is not a mere description of the given but also a questioning about the givenness of the given, it involves a reflecting attitude of

to something which is not the reflecting subject but which it tries to „reach" and to „grasp". Cognition, therefore, can be figuratively described as the „getting hold" by the intellect of something other than itself, something that exists independently of it[129]. This independent or transcendent entity can become given to the intellect as soon as it directs its cognitive attention to it or may become given to the intellect through a continuing effort to know. But this entity may also remain cognitively inaccessible to the intellect, in other words, it may be altogether transintelligible[130].

Cognition starts with a state of mere passive awareness of something by the intellect, in which awareness the intellect only takes notice of the given, without elaborating on it. This is the non-thetic attitude[131] of the intellect. The mere passive awareness of the given is followed, in the process of cognition, by the subject's posing questions, tasks, and claims concerning the given. This is the thetic attitude of the intellect. Through the thetic attitude the given is articulated into data, and this articulation is a condition for further non-thetic expansion of the given. Thus the epistemological subject is not a mere mould which the cognisible fills and affects producing in it the data of the cognised but it is also an active entity[132]. It acts by anticipating the objects to be cognised and by directing its cognitive attention to them[133]. It also acts by articulating the given into data, by arranging the notions thus obtained into logical and empirical relations, and by surmising what the transcendent object may be and how it may relate to the given. The thetic attitudes of the intellect involve also emotive and conative acts. Performing these acts in the process of cognition, the intellect exhibits itself as being a mode of *the mind:* the entity whose essence is to perform cognitive, emotive and conative acts.

The above contrasting of the given with the transcendent object of cognition suggests that the structure of the epistemological relation is more complex than was indicated above. It appears that instead of one epistemological object there are two: the immanent object and the transcendent object. To avoid the dual construction of the epistemological object, which appears to entail a multiplication of epistemological problems, the given can be construed as a determination, a mode of the subject. The „increase" of the given in the process of cognition is thus

---

the intellect, and is thus characterised by the *intentio obliqua*. Cf. the *intentio recta* of ontology as described *supra* s. 5.

129 Cf. the views on this matter of John Anderson stated concisely in his article cited *supra* n. 127.

130 See Hartmann, op. cit. 204–208.

131 On this notion see J. P. Sartre: L'Etre et le Néant, 41st ed. 1953, 16–23.

132 Cf. Descartes: Meditationes de Prima Philosophia, Meditatio Tertia; E. Husserl: Méditations Cartesiennes, 1931, 118; Lewis, op. cit. ch. i, esp. p. 17.

133 Cf. Russell: Human Knowledge, 439 ff.; F. Kaufmann: Methodenlehre der Sozialwissenschaften, 1934, 124.

an articulation of the intellect. It neither involves that the epistemological object, that is, the transcendent object, „penetrates" into the subject nor that the epistemological subject „merges" into the object. Like any other entity, the given, too, can become an object of cognitive attention and efforts, that is, it can become an epistemological object. This given is, however, a past state of the intellect and as such is transcendent to the intellect, which cognises it as a given that *was* given.

Corresponding to the ontological distinctions of the entities there are three principal types of cognition[134]: perception, reflection, and intellection. Perception is the cognition of hyletic entities[135]. The instruments of perceptive cognition are. the senses, which operate on the states of physical-material being (the so-called „outer" senses: seeing hearing, etc.), or of organic or psychic being („inner" „senses": mechanisms registering pain, fatigue, anxiety, etc.). Reflection is the cognition of noëtic entities[136]. The instruments of reflective cognition are acts of thinking operating on thoughts. Intellection is the cognition of eidetic entities. The instruments of intellective cognition are acts of thinking operating on abstractions of thought.

The given exists in the positive modes of distinctness and clarity[137] and in the negative modes of indistinctness and unclarity. The given is distinct if a datum is articulated in its relations to other data so that the intellect can identify it as a particular entity among the totality of what is given to the intellect. The given is clear if all the elements of a datum and their relations to each other are distinctly apprehended by the intellect. Insofar as the given is neither clearly nor distinctly given it is intuitively given. Intuitions thus always lack in clarity and distinctness, but they nevertheless can be keen, unmistakable. Cognising intuitively, the intellect is unaware of both the intrinsic and extrinsic relations of a datum, but it still recognises this datum as a unit of thoughts, as an undifferentiated whole of them. Insofar as the given is distinctly or clearly given, it is rationally given. To cognise rationally is to comprehend. To cognise intuitively is to understand. „To apprehend" is used in the present inquiry as a common name for „to comprehend[138]" and „to understand".

In the subject sphere there is an open possibility of thetic occurrences by which a datum enters into relations with other data. Some of these relations have a transcending character referring to something beyond

---

[134] On the types of cognition see C. Stumpf: Erkenntnislehre, 1939, vol. I, pp. 207–371.

[135] On the status of the perceptive and reflective cognition in human experience see S. Alexander: Space, Time, and Deity, 3rd impr. 1950, vol. I, p. 4 ff., 29, 41 ff.

[136] Cf. Lewis, op. cit. 24 ff.

[137] On clear and distinct cognition cf. the classical statement of Descartes: Regulae de Inquirenda Veritate. For a comment thereon see A. Boyce Gibson: The Philosophy of Descartes, 1932, 151 ff.

[138] On the use of the words „to apprehend" and „to comprehend" cf. Alexander, op. cit. I, p. 42.

the givenness of the cogniser's mind. They assert that this object is such or such, or that with respect to this object something is the case. Whether that which these references assert is actually the case or not the case, the intellect can, of course, only assume. The principles by recourse to which this assumption is made are the criteria of truth, or — to use a more accurate even though a less attractive phrase — the criteria of trueness. These criteria are provided by the norms (rules[139]) specifying the conditions of the attribution of the value „true" to a belief[140]. They are reasons by recourse to which beliefs are substantiated as true or false. The circumstance residing in a belief which makes the value „true" attributable to it is truth-conformity. The circumstance which founds the validity of the judgment that a belief has trueness is the correspondence of this belief to the assumed transcendent actualities about which the assertion is made by the belief. What this correspondence means is a matter of speculation on which hardly any essential epistemological problem depends.

The principal criteria of trueness[141] are consistency, theoretical productivity, pragmatic capacity, and evidence. A belief is consistent if it is not contradictory, that is, if that which it asserts is compatible with any other belief which the intellect has accepted as true. A belief has theoretical productivity if it serves as a basis for achieving practical ends of the intellect. A belief is evident if the intellect apprehends that it is impossible to accept the opposite of this belief as true[142]. The reason by which the validity of the criteria of trueness is ultimately substantiated is the fact that they have proved to be indispensable for man's orientation in the world and for the achievement of his ends. The test as to whether a belief has the character of trueness appears to be never absolutely conclusive; verification is a never-ending process[143]. It does not provide absolute certainty.

---

139 Cf. J. Dewey: Theory of Valuation, 1939, 20 ff.

140 For the arguments that the true is a value see L. Lavelle: Traité des Valeurs, 1955, vol. II, p. 349. See also Lewis, op. cit. 10: „Knowledge is not a descriptive but a normative category." And see A. Sesonske: Cognitive and Normative, 1956, 17, Philosophy and Phenomenological Research, 1, at 8 ff.; R. M. Chisholm: Epistemic Statements and Ethics of Belief, 1956, 16, Philosophy and Phenomenological Research, 447—460.

141 On the criteria of trueness see Hartmann: Grundzüge, 427—444; I. Tammelo: Untersuchungen zum Wesen der Rechtsnorm, 1947, 24—29; S. E. Toulmin: The Place of Reason in Ethics, 1950, 95; S. Alexander: Space, Time, and Deity, 3rd impr. 1950, vol II, p. 251 ff.

142 Cf. F. H. Bradley: Appearance and Reality, 9th impr. 1930: „The criterion of truth may be called inconceivability of the opposite ... Now the impossible may either be absolute or relative, but can never be directly based on our impotence ... In the end, one has to say, ‚I must not', because I am unable but because I am prevented." On the problem of evidence see especially E. Husserl: Ideen zu einer reinen Phänomenologie und phänomenologischen Philosophie, 3rd impr. 1928, 282—303. See also M. Farber: The Foundation of Phenomenology, 1943, 444—447.

143 See Lewis, op. cit. 191 ff.

The view that absolute certainty is not attainable in cognition imports an epistemological skepsis[144]. The above considerations give, however, no reason to accept Pyrrhonic skepsis, according to which there is no reason to believe that one assertion is true and other is not, and that one course of action is wiser than the other[145]. Formulating the position of skepticism in the proposition: „Everything is doubtful", this assertion is a paralogism because it applies also to itself, and in self-inclusion says that it is doubtful that everything is doubtful. This does not, of course, prove that there is something absolutely certain for the intellect, but it shows that consistent skepticism gives no licence to the Pyrrhonic arrogance[146].

8. The Epistemological Aspect of Justice

Since Knowing is embedded in Being, the clarification of the epistemological aspect of justice presupposes the awareness of certain ontological features of justice, justness, the just, and the idea of justice, which features determine the types and modes of the cognition of justice. According to the ontological analysis of justice attempted in section 6 above, justice and the idea of justice as actualities are ontic entities, whereas justness and the just are eidetic entities. As possibilities they are all eidetic entities. By their structure, justice and the idea of justice are complex entities, whereas justness and the just are simple entities. Within the domain of ontic being, justice as an actuality has hyletic being and the idea of justice as an actuality has noëtic being.

That justice as an actuality has hyletic being does not, of course, mean that it is completely dissolvable into spatial-temporal components. Since justice has the eidetic entity „justness" for one of its elements and, as any entity, it must have also certain formal characters, it has an eidetic aspect. The ontic aspect of justice consists in the rules according to which a situation is deemed to have justness, in the act or acts of the attribution of the just to this situation, and in the circumstances which make the object of attribution a social situation. A social situation implies that there is a plurality of entities communicating with each other and able to behave according to the rules providing criteria of justness. Hence it appears that for the cognition of justice all types and kinds of cognition are required[147]: Justness as a character of justice is an eidetic entity, and

---

[144] For related viewpoints see A. N. Whitehead: Essays in Science and Philosophy, 1947, 95; Bradley, op. cit. viii; Lavelle: Traité, II, p. 361 ff.

[145] See B. Russell: Sceptical Essays, 1948, 11–13.

[146] For objections to excessive skepticism and on mitigation of skepticism see Hume: An Inquiry concerning Human Understanding, s. XII, part ii and iii. See also I. Tammelo: Rational Man and Radical Doubt, 1953, passim. On the limits of skepticism in Descartes see Boyce Gibson, op. cit. p. 82 ff.

[147] With the argument that different types and modes of cognition are involved in the cognition of justice cf. C. I. Lewis: An Analysis of Knowledge and Valuation, 1946, 554: „Valuation is always a matter of empirical knowledge. But what is right and what is just, can never be determined by empirical facts alone."

therefore is cognised by intellection. The rules providing criteria of justness as rules existing *hic et nunc* are noëtic entities, and therefore are cognised by reflection. The acts of the attribution of the just are psychic events, and therefore are cognised by „inner“ perception. The manifested behaviour of the members of a society in which justice is realised is a physical occurrence, and therefore is cognised by „outer“ perception. The idea of justice, being a notion, is cognised by reflection. The cognition of its eidetic aspects, of course, involves intellection. There is no perception involved in the cognition of the idea of justice insofar as it is to be apprehended as an idea. The existence of this idea in the mind is, however, founded on psychical events, which are cognised by „inner“ perception. Justice and the idea of justice, being eidetic entities, are cognised by intellection.

Although the type of cognition of justness and the just, likewise the type of cognition of justice and the idea of justice as possibilities, is intellection, this cognition appears not to be unsupported by a perception of ontic entities[148]. Justness is cognised when the act of attribution of the just has been performed and the object of attribution has appeared in the „light“ or „mood[149]“ of this attribute. Thus the intellection of justness presupposes reflective or perceptive cognition of the entity deemed to have justness and a reflection of the notion of the corresponding act. The same holds, *mutatis mutandis,* for the cognition of the just. Although the type of cognition of the just as such is intellection, this cognition is actually supported by reflective and perceptive acts performed to cognise the ontic embodiment of the just[150], which embodiment is a specific emotive-conative state of the mind. The ontic entities whose perception supports the intellection of justice and the idea of justice as possibilities, are justice and the idea of justice as actualities. This intellection involves going beyond the respective actualities by eliminating certain elements of them, by adding certain other elements to them which may not be encountered in the actuality in view, and by combining all elements thus obtained into unities to which no actuality corresponds. So it can be said that although justice and the idea of justice as possibilities have an ontological priority over justice and the idea of justice as actualities, the latter have an eptstemological priority over the former.

To apprehend justice, justness, the just, and the idea of justice in the mode of distinct cognition, these entities must be apprehended as

---

148 It is not a pure *„Wesenserschauung“*. On the method of *Wesenserschauung* see E. Husserl: Erfahrung und Urteil (ed. by L. Landgrebe, 1948), 410–421. See also A. Reinach: Was ist Phänomenologie? 1951, passim.

149 Cf. L. Lavelle: Traité des Valeurs, 1955, vol. II, p. 476.

150 On the cognition of values see generally W. M. Urban: Valuation, Its Nature and Laws, 1909, 21–54; E. W. Hall: What Is Value? 1952, 63–112; A. Meinong: Psychologisch-ethische Untersuchungen zur Werttheorie, 1894, Part I, ch. i; Ch. Ehrenfels: System der Werttheorie, 1897, vol. I, ch. i; M. Scheler: Der Formalismus in der Ethik und die materiale Wertethik, 4th ed. 1954, 669, and references in the Index *sub voce „Werterkenntnis“*. See also V. Kraft: Die Grundlagen einer wissenschaftlichen Wertlehre, 1937, 3 ff.

having determined relations to all other entities. To apprehend justice, justness, the just, and the idea of justice in the mode of clear cognition, they must be apprehended also in their intrinsic relations, that is, the elements of their structure and the relations of these elements to each other must be determined. The just as a distinct entity is cognised by apprehending it in relation to other adherent qualities with which it appears to have a similarity and with which it is often confused. These qualities are the equitable and the lawful, but also the true, the correct, the right, and the good. A distinct knowledge of the just means also a distinct knowledge of justness, which is the counterpart of the attribute „just" in inherent being. Justice as a distinct entity is apprehended by confronting it with other social situations, especially with equity and legality. The idea of justice as a distinct entity is apprehended by confronting it with the ideas of these situations. It appears that for a distinct knowledge of justice and the idea of justice, a distinct knowledge of the just and of justness is a precondition. Since justice is an entity of a complex structure, a rational knowledge of it in the sense of both distinct and clear knowledge is possible. The same holds for the idea of justice. In contrast to justice and the idea of justice, a clear knowledge of the just and justness appears not to be possible at all. Both are, as it was shown in section 6 above, entities of simple structure. Their „inner" aspect can thus be only intuitively apprehended[151].

Although justice and the idea of justice are amenable to comprehension to a fuller extent than justness and the just, intuition is nevertheless the original mode in which even they are given to the intellect. Rational knowledge of them is obtained through thetic acts operating on their intuitive givenness, which exists non-thetically. The non-thetic awareness, in which their intuitions consist, first arises when the intellect is confronted with situations which it considers unjust[152]. This is a special case of what appears to be a general feature of the cognition of values: the consciousness of values arises through the experiencing of obstacles to the subject's value strivings. The intuitive apprehension of justice is sufficient for the ordinary purposes of man's life. Recognition of justness and the just as distinct from justice and apprehension of the idea of justice as an entity distinct from justice, justness, and the just, is the first essential step in the rational penetration into the vague and confused entity called „justice". The analysis of justice leading to its distinct and clear knowledge takes place mainly on

[151] This is what Julius Stone implies when he says that the just „as a value may only be capable of being indicated by statements of its use or by statements pointing out the concrete contexts in which its content may be seen". See his treatise: Legal Controls of International Conflict, 1954, 53 ff. On the apprehension of the entities of simple structure see Hall, op. cit. 3.

[152] For the argument that injustice has a cognitive priority over justice see E. N. Cahn: The Sense of Injustice, 1949, esp. p. 15 ff. See also A. E. Sutherland: The Law and One Man among Many, 1956, 72–74, who discusses this view of Cahn in a section entitled „Injustice perceived by indignation".

the scholarly level. Its beginnings exist, however, already in the ordinary thinking reflected in the usage of the corresponding terms in language.

The problem of truth in relation to justice, justness, the just, and the idea of justice involves the question, How are the assertions about them and their elements to be verified? Analytical propositions such as „The just is an entity" and „Justice exists" are verifiable by recourse to the criterion of evidence. Their truth is founded on the evident assumption that evertyhing is an entity and everything, except the All (the Absolute), exists (the All being the entity that only subsists). The verification of the empirical propositions such as „This law does not promote justice" and „This man is just" occurs by recourse to the criterion of consistency. This criterion requires that there is no proposition substantiated as true which contradicts the propositions the verfication of which is sought. Theoretical assertions of non-analytical nature concerning justice, justness, the just, and the idea of justice (for example, „Justness is an inherent quality", „Justice is a social situation", „The idea of justice is cognised by reflective acts") are verified in addition to the application of the criteria of evidence and consistency, also by recourse to the criteria of theoretical productivity and pragmatic capacity.

IV. Logical Considerations

9. On the Principles of Logic and Semantics

In the attempts to acquire and to secure knowledge, certain principles are employed according to which the beliefs are organised into a uniform and consistent whole and according to which the beliefs are handled as belonging to such whole. These principles constitute the subject matter of logic. They enable the intellect to apprehend the data as distinct and clear notions, to link them with each other, and to group them together so that knowledge may become transparent, surveyable, and better communicable. The principles of logic are involved also in the comprehension of justice, and they belong to the fundamentals of justice[153].

---

[153] Pure logic (as distinguished from the methodologies of particular sciences) rests on the idea of *mathesis universalis,* according to which the given has a basic rational structure apprehensible by means of uniform relations of universal applicability. On this idea see E. Husserl: Formale und transzendentale Logik, 1929, 64 ff.; N. Hartmann: Zur Grundlegung der Ontologie, 3rd ed. 1948, 293 ff.; O. Bondy: Logical and Epistemological Problems in Legal Philosophy, 1951, 29, Australasian Journal of Philosophy, 81, at 83; I. Tammelo: Legal Dogmatics and the Mathesis Universalis, 1948, 3.

The scope of logic is assumed to extend to the whole realm of the knowable. This does not, however, mean that everything actually is or must be logically determinable, but that logical determinations may be sought wherever thought penetrates. All questions about logic itself transcend the scope of logic. They are an object of transcendental logic, which is epistemology and ontology applied to logical entities and to the entity „logic" itself. On formal and transcendental logic see Husserl, op. cit., passim.

The central concern of logic is to provide instruments for correct reasoning, or to use a less apt but more current expression, for formally true reasoning[154]. Formal (or analytical) truth is to be distinguished from truth in the proper sense, which is not a peculiar concern of logic but of epistemology. There is, however, a connection between these two kinds of truth: Logic, striving for self-consistent or *correct* knowledge, is a most important agent in the attainment of true and founded beliefs. From true premisses it helps to develop true conclusions, and for false propositions it helps to trace the source of falsity[155]. The regulative principle peculiar to logic is thus the idea of what is deemed to have correctness. This principle is actualised in the reasoning that is in accordance with the norms providing the criteria of correctness[156], which in logic are the counterpart of what in epistemology are the norms providing the criteria of trueness[157]. The norms providing the criteria of correctness occur as the rules of concept formation, inference, and classification.

There appears to be a close connection between logic and language. Grammatical and syntactical principles have a similarity to logical principles[158], and the connectives which modern logic employs for constituting its basic relations (conjunction, disjunction, implication, etc.) are linguistic entities in a certain respect. But there is no thoroughgoing dependence between language and logic; they largely concur but do not coincide. Language, being a means of communication between individual minds must have features which are not exclusively private to each individual mind but common to everyone. The uniformity of the structure of language tends to take logical forms. The logical relations brought to expression assume philological forms. For the inquiry into logical principles, language thus constitutes an important basis, because in language these principles are embodied to a large extent[159].

The basic entities on which and with which logic operates are notions. The notions in logic occur as statements and as concepts. The statement is a thetic datum consisting of at least three notions: it is a relation constituted by the subject and the predicate as two relata, and the copula as the relator. These three elements are at least implicit in every occurrence of a statement, although they need not be explicit in the sentences by which statements are expressed[160]. The principal kinds of

---

[154] L. Wittgenstein: Philosophical Investigations (transl. G. E. M. Anscomb, 1953), 42, § 89.

[155] As in epistemology, the attitude of the mind engaged in logical inquiries is *intentio obliqua*.

[156] On the criteria („tests") of correctness see C. I. Lewis: An Analysis of Knowledge and Valuation, 1946, 111 ff.

[157] See *supra* s. 7.

[158] On the relations of logic and language cf. R. Carnap: The Logical Syntax of Language, 1947; A. J. Ayer: Language, Truth and Logic, 1948.

[159] See B. Russell: An Inquiry into Meaning and Truth, 3rd impr. 1948 esp. pp. 30—47.

[160] See I. Tammelo: Sketch for a Symbolic Juristic Logic, 1956, 8, Journal of Legal Education, 277, at 283, n. 36.

statements are indicative, interrogative, imperative, optative, and putative statements. Indicative statements are called propositions[161]. Non-indicative statements[162] may be called precations[163]. Propositions, for example, „This man is just", „There is no justice", state (indicate) that something is or is not the case. So with respect to propositions the question whether they are true or false appears to be proper[164]. Precations, for example, „Is this behaviour just?", „Be just!", „May justice be done!", „Suppose it were just!", state (invite) that something is or is not to be made the case[165], in other words, they tell someone to bring something about. Statements, like all the acts of the intellect, are characterised by in-tentionality[166], which means the mental contents' referring to (or being directed to) a certain object. With propositions this object is what is indicated to be[167], with precations this object is what is invited to be. The object which an interrogative in-tends is an answer to its question. The object which an imperative in-tends is compliance with its demand. The object which an optative in-tends is fulfilment of its wish. And the

---

161 On the view that not all statements are propositions see A. Ross: Towards a Realistic Jurisprudence, 1946, 97 ff.

162 With this classification of statements cf. W. G. Becker: Die Realität des Rechts (II), 1952, 40, Archiv für Rechts- und Sozialphilosophie, 375, at 398 ff.; I. Tammelo: Untersuchungen zum Wesen der Rechtsnorm, 1947, 30–33.

163 The absence of a single term covering all kinds of non-indicative statements has been an embarrassement of discussion in this area. For the suggestion that I use the therm „precation" I am indebted to Professor Julius Stone. I am also again grateful to Jaan Puhvel who has supplied Professor Stone's suggestion with the following learned note on the linguistic aspect of the term:

„The Indo-European root _*prek̑-_ has the early meaning ‚to ask' in both interrogative (‚to question') and voluntative sense (‚to demand'): Sanskrit _prā́ś-_ ‚(legal) inquiry', but Latin _preces_ ‚requests, prayers' (_precor_ ‚I entreat, pray'; _procus_ ‚suitor'; cf. Lithunian _pir̃šti_ ‚to woo'). A radical verbal form is seen in the Vedic aorist _áprāt_ ‚he asked', while the present is generally formed with an _-sk-_ suffix: Skt. _pr̥ccháti,_ Armenian _harçanem_ ‚ask'; Latin _poscō_ < _*pr̥k̑-skō_ ‚demand'; Old High German _forscōn_ ‚seek, inquire'; an iterative present type is seen in Lith. _prašýti,_ Old Slavonic _prositi_ ‚ask, demand' (also Old Latin supine _procitum_ in Livius Andronicus); cf. further Gothic _fraíhnan,_ Old Saxon _frāgōn_ ‚ask, question'."

164 Cf. Wittgenstein, op. cit. 52, § 136: „What _engages_ with the concept of truth . . . is a proposition."

165 Cf. R. M. Hare: The Language of Morals, 1952, 5, 17–31. Cf. also S. E. Toulmin: The Place of Reason in Ethics, 1950, 50 ff.

166 On the notion of in-tentionality see E. Husserl: Logische Untersuchungen, 1922, vol. II, part i, pp. 364 ff. See also H. B. Veatch: Intentional Logic, 1952, esp. pp. 78, 396; A. Gurvitsch: On the Intentionality of Consciousness, in M. Farber (ed.): Philosophical Essays in Memory of Edmund Husserl, 1940, 65–83; M. Farber: The Foundation of Phenomenology, 1943, 333–387; R. M. Chisholm: Intentionality and the Theory of Signs, 1952, 3, Philosophical Studies, 56–63.

167 Cf. A. Pap: Elements of Analytical Philosophy, 1949, 482.

object which a putative in-tends is acceptance of what it assumes. In contrast to propositions, precations do not appear to have conformity to the attribute „true". Their specific attribute is the right[168]. An interrogative is deemed to have rightness if it satisfies the accepted standards of admissibility concerning questions, an imperative is deemed to have rightness if it satisfies such standards concerning commands, an optative is deemed to have rightness if it satisfies those concerning wishes, and a putative is deemed to have rightness if it satisfies those concerning the making of assumptions.

The concept is a non-thetic[169] datum formed by means of a statement or statements. It has two aspects: connotation and denotation. Connotation indicates the relations which the concept has to other notions, whereas denotation indicates the field of objects which the concept embraces. For example, the connotation of the concept „triangle" indicates that it is a figure, a geometrical figure, and a geometrical figure constituted by three intersecting lines; the denotation of the same concept, however, indicates that it embraces as instances „isoceles", „rectangular triangle", „spheric triangle", etc. There are concepts which denote only an individual entity (for example, „Sokrates", „the Trojan horse"); they are individual concepts. The concepts which denote a plurality of entities are general concepts. On the other hand there are concepts whose connotation has only one single determinant (for example, „blue", „this[170]"); they are simple concepts. The concepts whose connotation consists of a plurality of determinants are complex concepts. A concept which would have no determinant for its connotation is inconceivable. There appear to be, however, concepts with „zero extensions" in the sense that they do not denote any hyletic actuality (for example, „a flying horse", „Utopia"). The emptiness of these concepts is only empirical[171]; denoting a mere possibility they are evidently denoting something and cannot be without a denotation. Where there is not even a possible in-tentional object for a pretended concept (for example, „a square circle", „a green sound"), there is no concept at all but only an aggregate of incompatible notions. Concepts can ordinarily be analysed in terms of propositions[172]. There appear to be concepts, preëminently the ontological categories, which cannot be analysed into propositions only but require precations for their analysis: they can be regarded as being essentially *con-cepta* of statements whose in-tentional object is what is invited to be.

---

[168] For a similar conception see E. W. Hall: What Is Value? 1952, 110–112, 189 ff., 237 ff. Hall employs the term „legitimate" in the same sense as „right" is employed in the present context. Cf. M. White: Toward Reunion in Philosophy, 1956, 259. For an analysis of the notion „right" cf. Hare, op. cit. 151–162.

[169] With the terms „thetic" and „non-thetic" cf. Hare's terms „neustic" and „phrastic" (see Hare, op. cit. 8) which seem to serve a somewhat similar function.

[170] On the concept „this" see Russell, op. cit. 108–115.

[171] Cf. Tammelo, article cited *supra* n. 160, p. 288.

[172] See ibid. 284–287.

Statements which have concepts for their components can be employed as premisses for inferences. There are two principal modes of inference: direct and indirect. In the former a single statement itself is a sufficient basis for the inference, in the latter two or more statements are required for an inference to be drawn. In traditional logic the modi of conclusions[173] have been applied only to propositions. It appears, however, that precations, too, have a capacity of logical expansion, permitting certain inferences to be drawn from them[174].

The approach to logic from the side of language raises the problem of the semantic acts. The analysis of these acts is a task of semantics. A semantic act may be analysed into *signum* (sign, symbol, or expression), a *significatum* (sense or reference), and a *designatum* (meaning or the referred[175]). The *signum* is a spatial-temporal event conveying notions of one intellect to another. In ordinary language, words, phrases, and sentences function as *signa*[176]. The *significatum* is the notion or the noëtic object conveyed by the *signum*[177]. The *designatum* is the entity or the noëmatic object[178] to which a *significatum* refers. This referring-to is a peculiar circumstance characterising all mental acts; it is the so-called in-tentionality. In a complete semantic act a *signum* signifies something, a *significatum* refers to, means, or designates something, and a *designatum* is designated, meant, or referred to by a *signum* or a *significatum*. There are two types of incomplete semantic acts: (1) When *signa* do not signify anything at all in a given situation. In this case nothing is also designated, meant, or referred to, and the *signa* are senseless[179] (for example, collocations of sounds or letters such as „rptmk" or „aeiouy" accidentally placed together). All senseless *signa* are obviously also meaningless and *vice versa*. (2) When *significata* do not refer to, mean, or designate anything which is at least a possibility. In that case the *significata* and their corresponding *signa* are absurd[180] (for example, „a square circle",

---

[173] On the problem of the modi of conclusions see A. Pfänder: Logik, 1929, 36 ff., 133 ff.

[174] See Tammelo, article cited supra n. 160, p. 289.

[175] For analysis of the semantic act see H. Leblanc: Positions and Propositions on Universals, 1951, 12, Philosophy and Phenomenological Research, 95–104; Husserl, op. cit. 23 ff., 61 ff. See also C. K. Ogden and I. A. Richards: The Meaning of Meaning, 10th ed. 1949; H. Lipps: Untersuchungen zu einer hermeneutischen Logik, 1938.

[176] In the present inquiry the word „term" is ordinarily used for the signum of a notion and the word „sentence" is used for the *signum* of a statement.

[177] On the distinction of *significatum* and notion see Lewis, op. cit. ch. vi, in whose terminology „*significatum*" is „linguistic meaning" and „notion" is „sense meaning".

[178] On noësis and noëma see E. Husserl: Ideen zu einer reinen Phänomenologie und phänomenologischen Philosophie, 3rd. impr. 1928, 179–201.

[179] On the need for a distinction between meaning and being true see H. L. A. Hart: A Logician's Fairy Tale, 1951, 60, Philosophical Review, 198, esp. at 204.

[180] Or – to use a term of C. I. Lewis – „self-inconsistent". See Lewis, op. cit. 115, n. 3.

„a whispering silence[181]". *Signa* may have more than one *significatum*, in which case they are equivocal or homonymous (for example, „see", „means", „let"). On the other hand, *designata* may be referred to by different *significata* signified by various *signa*, in which case these *signa* and *significata* are equivalent or synonomous (for example, „equilateral triangle" and „equiangular triangle", „the evening star" and „the morning star", „twice two" and „five minus one").

The aspect of the semantic act which falls into the ambit of logic appears to be *significatum*[182]. *Signa* are but vehicles carrying logical operations in the course of communication between intellects. If *signa* are thought of by an intellect, they cease to be *signa* but become *designata*. *Designata* are of no direct concern for logic either. They are the objects which to apprehend or to affect in man's contemplative or practical life, logic is employed as an *organon*.

The ideal of logic is to provide a completely rational, self-consistent system of all notions. As such it is expected to be free from contradictions. This ideal, however, does not appear to have been attained by any logic. In a certain stage of its application paradoxes emerge, which are irremovable on the same level of logic. They may be dealt with in a superordinate system of logic, in which, however, paradoxes peculiar to it emerge, and so *ad infinitum*. Logical paradoxes occur if a concept or proposition is such that it implies both itself and its negation. Ontological notions are instances of the occurrence of logical paradoxes. Thus „Being" denotes its negation „Non-being" and „Something" denotes its negation „Nothing". Such notions are irrational, paralogical[183] by their very nature. Yet they are something more than what is signified by senseless (and meaningless) *signa* and what is meant by absurd *significata*. They are founded on intuitions which a thinker who thinks of the fundamentals of reality cannot leave unrecognised, and they appear to be indispensable for any consistent thinking which tries to apprehend these fundamentals[184].

---

[181] Absurd *significata* should be distinguished from metaphorical references, for example, „weighing the evidence", „mansions of justice", „the shepherd and guardian of Being". These references are not devoid of content but may be pregnant with it. They need not even be empirically empty like, for example, „phoenix" and „ectoplasm".

[182] Many modern logicians, wielding the Occam's Razor, have seen a possibility of excluding the *significatum* from the use of logic as an unnecessary entity and correlating the *signa* and *designata* directly with each other. See, for example, R. Carnap: Einführung in die symbolische Logik, 1954, 7, 16. In my opinion this leads to some artificial constructions and unnecessary complications in logical reasoning. What may seem theoretically simpler need not always be simpler in applications of theory.

[183] On the problem of the paralogical see R. Heiss: Logik des Widerspruchs, 1932. For a *locus classicus* on paralogisms see Kant: Kritik der reinen Vernunft, 1787, 448—595.

[184] The paralogical can safely said to be nonsense only if a narrow criterion of „sense" is employed, for example, the criterion of empirical verifiability. For a critical evaluation of this criterion see White, op. cit ch. vi, esp. p. 109. It is more accurate to say that the paralogical is non-sense, that

10. The Logical Aspect of Justice

When the principles discussed in the previous section are applied to the problem of justice, the following can be said about the semantic aspect of justice: „Justice“ in its enveloping sense is an equivocation. In the Second Discourse and in section 6 of the present inquiry an attempt was made to render the word „justice“ univocal by using it only to signify a social situation and by employing the words „justness“, „the just“, and „the idea of justice“ for its other *significata*. All these *signa* signify something and all the corresponding *significata* designate at least possibilities. In the light of the analysis carried out in the previous sections, the *designata* (noëmatic objects) of „justice“ (properly so called), „justness“, „the just“, and „the idea of justice“ appear to be such that their concepts would have the following logical features:

The concept „justice“ appears to be a complex concept because it connotes a social situation. A social situation is always a relation: there are at least three elements to compose it: person P, person P_1, and the social nexus which unities them in a social group. A further reason why „justice“ is to be considered a complex concept is that in its connotation there is also the relation of an attribution, namely the attribution of the just to a social situation. On the other hand, the concept of justice appears to be a general concept. It denotes an indeterminate number of social situations eventuating in an indeterminate space-time, to which situations the just is attributed in an indeterminate number of the acts of attribution. The denotation of „justice“ contains not only the actualities of justice but also the possibilities of justice.

In contrast to the concepts of justice, the concepts of justness and the just appear to be simple and individual concepts. The noëmatic object of neither of them appears to be analysable into elements; these objects are substratal as „blueness“ and „the blue“, „coldness“ and „the cold“, „fragrance“ and „the fragrant“ appear to be in the field of sensory qualities[185]. Neither the concept of justness nor the concept of the just refers to a plurality of entities. Their noëmatic objects are sometimes altogether unique, that is, these objects are eidetic individualities[186]. The fact that „justness“ and „the just“ are conceived by a plurality of concrete intellects does not make, of course, their concepts general. The individuality of a concept is solely determined by the uniqueness of the noëmatic object to which this concept refers. Further, the fact that the noësis of justness and of the just eventuate in a great variety of shadings

---

is, something to which no sense-experience corresponds. The paralogical is admittedly irrational; it is beyond rational apprehension. It is, however, not beyond the scope of reasonable handling. Reasonable attitude with regard to the paralogical does not appear to be ceasing to wonder about it or being silent about it but rather investigating the circumstances of its existence and its implications in order to learn thus everything that can be learnt about the dangers into which its *aporiae* may lure the thinker.

[185] See J. Stone: Legal Controls of International Conflict, 1954, 53.

[186] On the concept of „eidetic individuality“ cf. E. Husserl: Erfahrung und Urteil, 1948, 460–471.

need not be regarded as abolishing the uniqueness of their corresponding noëmata. The individual variations of the mind's experiences ought to be regarded as attempts to „reach" in-tentionally noëmata, each of which exists in its uniqueness in the realm of eidetic Being as a *limes* towaros which the apprehending intellect cognitively strives with a greater or lesser success.

The concept of the idea of justice is a complex and general concept. It is a complex concept because its connotation contains at least two determinants: „notion" and „justice", of which the latter is a complex concept itself. The concept of the idea of justice is a general concept because it denotes a plurality of notions occurring in an indeterminate number of actual and possible minds (my idea of justice, your idea of justice, his idea of justice, the idea of justice entertained by person P).

The principles discussed in the previous sections of the present inquiry supply also a basis for clarification of the logical character of the norms that provide criteria of justness: they make it possible to analyse the norms according to which situations, persons, or behaviour are deemed to have justness or the just is attributed to these situations, persons, or this behaviour. The primary form of such a norm appears to be: „X, be Y (in order that you may be deemed to have justness)!" Another way of presenting the same norm is: „X ought to be Y (in order that he may be deemed to have justness)[187]." The latter statement is an assertion about the existence of a command, the compliance with which the above imperative statement in-tends[188]. As the statement „X ought to be Y (. . .)" is a proposition, the question whether it is true or false can properly be raised concerning it. The primary form of a norm providing a criterion of justness (that is, „X, be Y (. . .)!") does not, however, allow this question to be asked. It raises only the question of its rightness, which may be founded on its being an inference from a wider principle relating to justness (for example, „Everyone who has the character a, be Y!", „X has the character a", consequently „X, be Y!") or which may be founded on its being an evident statement. Apart from the propositions formed by the copula „ought to", there is another way of referring, in the propositional form, to the command, the compliance with which an imperative „in-tends", namely by employing the deontic mode „obligatory"[189]. In many cases, „X ought to be Y (. . .)" is equivalent to „Y is obligatory to X (. . .)". Thus instead of saying „X ought to be Y (in order that he may be deemed to have justness)" it

[187] On the problem of the „ought" see generally I. Tammelo: Sketch for a Symbolic Juristic Logic, 1956, 8, Journal of Legal Education, 277, at 290—292. Cf. A. N. Prior: The Ethical Copula, 1951, 29, Australasian Journal of Philosophy, 137—154; D. Grey: The Ethical Copula again, 1953, 31, ibid. 139—154. On the relations between „ought" and „imperatives" cf. R. M. Hare: The Language of Morals, 1952, 163—179.

[188] On the syntax of imperatives and other precations see E. W. Hall: What Is Value? 1952, 113—190.

[189] On deontic modes see H. von Wright: Deontic Logic, 1951, 60, Mind, 1—15; id.: An Essay on Modal Logic, 1951; Tammelo, article cited *supra* n. 187, pp. 288—290, 292—295.

may be said that „Y is obligatory to X (in order that he may be deemed to have justness)“. The latter proposition is a standard form of a norm[190] providing a criterion by reference to which human behaviour can be judged. It should be noted that „obligatory“ is compatible only with the attributes to which human behaviour conforms. So it would be absurd to say that „Y is obligatory to X (in order that X may be deemed to have correctness)“ To speak, however, in terms of „ought to“ of the latter kind of characters (for example, „M ought to be N in order that M may be deemed to have correctness)“ is by no means absurd.

In the imperative „X, be Y (in order that you may be deemed to have justness)!“, „X“ must designate an entity capable of being addressed in an imperative, whereas „Y“ must refer to a behaviour expected from X by the addresser[191]. Thus „Be Y!“ may mean either „Perform (or do) Y!“ or „Abstain from (or do not do) Y!“ If X performs Y or abstains from Y, he complies with the command of the norm providing a criterion of justness, and he or his behavior may rightly be deemed to have justness by reference to the criterion in question. „Non-just“ is equivalent to „either ‚unjust‘ or ‚neither-just-nor-unjust‘“. Since „justice“ (as an actuality) means a situation, it is obvious that the criteria of justness cannot directly be employed for determining an entity to be justice or not justice: an imperative cannot be addressed to a situation. However, the criteria of justness are applicable indirectly for determining whether a situation is justice or not justice, because social situations (which are situations conforming to the attribute „just“) have as one of their constituents the behavior of the entities which can be regarded as addressees of imperatives, that is, the behaviour of actual human beings.

If the attribution of the just to a behaviour occurs in accordance with a norm providing a criterion of justness, this attribution is right with reference to the criterion in question. The expression „is right“, like the phrase „is true“, is incomplete, and is employed to signify „is deemed to have rightness“. „Right“ and „wrong“, like „true“ and „false“, „correct“ and „incorrect“, etc. are adherent qualities (attributes). They are attributes in the „light“ or „mood“ of which certain

---

[190] The statement „Y is obligatory to X“ still preserves the character of being a norm. This character is preserved by the deontic mode „obligatory“ as its element. Because of this element the statement is not to be qualified as an „is“-statement. For arguments that norms are „ought“-statements see G. Nakhnikian: Professor Fuller on Legal Rules and Purpose, 1956, 2, Wayne Law Review, 190, at 201 and passim.

[191] Imperatives, like propositions, can be detached from the persons who are issuing them. Such imperatives are, to use a term of Karl Olivecrona, „independent imperatives“. They are to be distinguished from commands, to which a personal relation to the one who commands is constitutive. See K. Olivecrona: Law as a Fact, in P. Sayre (ed.), Interpretations of Modern Legal Philosophies, 1947, 542—577, at 546 ff.; id.: Der Imperativ des Gesetzes, 1942, 27 ff. According to Olivecrona, legal norms belong to the category of independent imperatives.

circumstances are „seen“ or „felt“ to have a certain character („trueness“, „correctness“, „justness“, etc.). It is clear that the norms according to which the right is attributed to an entity can be judged in reference to certain criteria. This leads to an infinite regress of the principles regulating the acts of attribution. This is nothing to be lamented but something to be accepted as one of the normal courses of philosophical thinking. The fact that philosophical reasoning, here as elsewhere, leads to *regressus in infinitum* does not mean that the philosopher ought to try ceaselessly to carry this regress out. He may stop at any time in his advance towards the receding horizon of philosophical vistas when at any stage of his movement he has no strength to continue or no interest in continuing[192].

V. Axiological Considerations

11. On Value and Validity

That justice stands in an intimate relation with the domain of values is a generally accepted view in legal and political philosophy. Thus an inquiry into the fundamentals of justice requires a clarification of the principles of values. The philosophical discipline whose concern it is to undertake this clarification is axiology or theory of values.

„Value“, as with many current philosophical terms, is an equivocation[193]. Its principal designata are: (1) an attribute, for example, the true, the bad, the just; (2) a character, for example, trueness, badness, justness; (3) a circumstance which has such a character, for example, truth, evil, justice. When „value“ designates an attribute it occurs in the subjective sense, that is, as an axiotic attribute. When „value“ designates a character it occurs in the transsubjective sense, that is, as an axiotic character. When „value“ designates a circumstance it occurs in the objective sense, that is, as an axiotic circumstance. It seems to be matter of subjective preference, which of the above should be regarded as value in the proper sense. Thus it is perhaps better to leave this question open and to use the word „value“ in an enveloping sense to designate any of the three above entities by this term when from the context it is obvious which of the three entities is meant. When there is, however, a danger of confusion, the more accurate expressions „axiotic attribute“, „axiotic character“, and „axiotic circumstance“ are to be used to remove the ambiguity of the word „value“[194].

---

[192] Cf. L. E. Thomas: Philosophic Doubt, 1955, 64, Mind, 333, at 340.

[193] On the homonymity of the word „value“ see L. Lavelle: Traité des Valeurs, 1953, vol. I, p. 3 ff. For rich references to relevant literature on the problem of values see this work as well as its second volume published in 1955. As leading contemporary works on values see also E. W. Hall: What Is Value? 1952; C. I. Lewis: An Analysis of Knowledge and Valuation, 1946; V. Kraft: Die Grundlagen einer wissenschaftlichen Wertlehre, 1937; N. Hartmann: Ethik, 3rd ed. 1949; M. Scheler: Der Formalismus in der Ethik und materiale Wertethik, 5th ed. 1954.

[194] In its narrow sense the notion „value“ denotes only positive values (for example, the good). In its wide sense it denotes also neutral values (the

Value as an axiotic attribute is not simply identical with adherent quality but with a special kind of this quality. An axiotic attribute is an attribute primarily experienced as an attitude or disposition by the mind performing emotive acts[195]. So it can assume a varying intensity; it can be „weighed" as against the other values, can enter into the relations of „more" and „most", „less" and „least"[196] with them. There are attributes which do not appear to be primarily experienced in emotive acts, and which are not „weighed", compared. These are non-axiotic attributes such as a thought attributed to a certain historical personality and a cause attributed to a certain event.

Axiotic attributes, like physical qualities, are qualities which apply to quantities, that is, to entities of which there is a greater or lesser extent of something, a higher or lower degree of something[197]. The grades of quantity of these entities are matched by the grades of axiotic intensity of values in the subjective sense. Thus apart from the good, there are also the better, the best, the less good, and the least good; apart from the ugly there are also the uglier, the ugliest, the less ugly and the least ugly; and apart from the just there are also the more just, the most just, the less just and the least just. The different grades of the axiotic intensity of the same value constitute a value-range. Thus „the least just — the less just — the just — the more just — the most just" is an example of this range. Another notable similarity which values have with physical qualities is their existence in three modes: positive, negative, and neutral[198]. The three modes of the same value constitute a value-type. Within every value-type there are positive values (the good, the right, the just), negative values (the bad, the wrong, the unjust), and neutral values (the neither-good-nor-bad, the neither-right-nor-wrong, the neither-just-nor-unjust) in the same way as there are physical qualities of the corresponding nature (for example, the black, the white, the neither-black-nor-white). Since there are grades of axiotic intensity with both positive and negative values, there are positive and negative value-ranges. It lies in the nature of the neutral value that it does not assume grades of axiotic intensity. The positive and negative value-ranges of the same value-type can be linked with each other through neutral value, in which case a complete value-range is formed. An example of such a value-range is „the best — the better — the good — the less good — the least good —

---

neither-good-nor-bad) and negative values or disvalues (the bad). In the present inquiry the term „value" is used in its wide sense mainly. Where it is used in its narrow sense, this should be obvious from the context.

[195] Cf. W. M. Urban: Valuation, Its Nature and Laws, 1909, 35 ff.; Lavelle, op. cit. I, pp. 188—196. Cf. also S. Alexander: Space, Time, and Deity, 3rd impr. 1950, vol. II, p. 243. And cf. Cicero: De Finibus, 5, 23, who conceives *iustitia* as *„animi affectio suum cuique tribuens"*.

[196] On comparative and superlative values thereby constituted see R. S. Perry: General Theory of Value, 1926, 19 ff., 597 ff.

[197] On the degrees of values cf. Lavelle, op. cit. II, p. 8, n. 1.

[198] On neutral values see Hartmann, op. cit. 613—620.

the neither-good-nor-bad — the least bad — the less bad — the bad — the worse — the worst".

On the basis of their structure, values can be divided into simple and complex values[199]. Simple values are values of substratal character (for example, the good, the wrong, the neither-true-nor-false) in the sense that they are not analysable into other values just as certain physical qualities (for example, the black, the hot, the bitter) cannot be analysed into other physical qualities. Complex values are values composed of a plurality of simple values[200]. For example, the sublime appears to be a unity of the good, the beautiful, and possibly other positive values; the loathsome appears to be a unity of the bad, the ugly, and possibly other negative values. Since simple values are irreducible to other values, one cannot say, for example, that the useful as an axiotic attribute is the beautiful and *vice versa,* even though the entity to which the value „useful" is attributed may have conformity to the beautiful and the entity to which the value „beautiful" is attributed may have conformity to the useful.

Values in the subjective sense, both simple and complex, are entities which, like all other entities, can be objects of axiotic attribution, through which specific axiotic circumstances (specific values in the objective sense) arise. In other words, values can be valuated[201]; they, too, have conformity to axiotic attributes. All positive values in the subjective sense can be graded as to their axiotic intensity[202] by the value of the values or the metavalue „high", and all negative values by the corresponding metavalue „low[203]". There is, of course, also a neutral metavalue, namely the neither-high-nor-low. The metavalues in the objective sense are „axiotic dignity" and „axiotic indignity". The value-ranges of the high and the low make it possible to apprehend the whole domain of values as organised in a hierarchical structure in which every value is given a certain place in the levels of axiotic dignity[204]. In a value-hierarchy there is an apex and counter-apex. The apex is occupied by the value which is apprehended as having the greatest axiotic dignity; the counter-apex is occupied by the value which is apprehended as having the greatest axiotic indignity. The supreme positive value may be named the *Summum Bonum*[205] and the supreme negative value the *Summum Malum,* considering that the good and the bad appear to be values of a universal axiotic pervasion[206], so that any entity whatsoever appears to have conformity to them. This

---

[199] On this distinction see G. Moore: Principia Ethica, 1929, 5—17.

[200] Cf. S. E. Toulmin: The Place of Reason in Ethics, 1950, 13—18.

[201] Cf. Lavelle, op. cit. I, pp. 320—322.

[202] On the problem of axiotic intensity cf. Perry, op. cit. 626—633, 642—644.

[203] On the „higher" and „lower" values cf. Scheler, op. cit. 107—120.

[204] On the hierarchical structure of the domain of values see Lavelle, op. cit. I, pp. 593—653; Hartmann, op. cit. 269—278; H. Reiner: Pflicht und Neigung, 1951, 168 ff.

[205] On the problem of the *Summum Bonum* cf. Perry, op. cit. 659—692.

[206] Cf. Lavelle, op. cit. II, p. 46.

feature of the good and the bad allows everything to be judged in relation to the Supreme Good and the Supreme Bad. The base of the hierarchy of positive values is occupied by all values which conform to the meta-value „high (simply)" whereas the base of the hierarchy of negative values is occupied by all values which conform to the metavalue „low (simply)". Between the base and the apex and the base and the counter-apex there is an indeterminate number of axiotic levels, higher or lower than the others occupied by values according to the degree of their axiotic dignity. The hierarchies of positive and negative values can be apprehended as being connected with each other by the plane of neutral values.

The attribution of values (in the subjective sense) to the objects of attribution and the constitution of axiotic circumstances thereby can be performed by reference to certain explicit or implicit principles, but it can also be completely unprincipled. In the former case the attribution and predication of values, or — to use an expression embracing both — valuation, is axiotically substantiated (or founded), in the latter case it is axiotically arbitrary. The principles on which valuations are founded are the criteria[207] of validity[208]. In the previous course of the present inquiry various types of these criteria have been already mentioned, especially the criteria of trueness and of correctness[209]. If a valuation is substantiated[210] by reference to the criteria of trueness, it is valid as true; if by reference to the criteria of correctness, it is

[207] These principles may be called „reasons". On „reasons" in prescriptive contexts see G. Nakhnikian: Professor Fuller on Legal Rules and Purpose, 1956, 2, Wayne Law Review, 190, at 198 ff. On the problem of criteria of valuation see R. M. Hare: The Language of Morals, 1952, 94—110.

[208] On the notion of validity see A. Liebert: Das Problem der Geltung, 1921; H. Rickert: System der Philosophie, 1921, vol. I, p. 115 ff.; V. Kraft, op. cit. 7; Lavelle, op. cit. I, 12 ff. On the problem of validity in connection with legal norms see O. Brusiin: Über das juristische Denken, 1951, 129 ff.

[209] On the nature of the criteria of validity cf. N. Hartmann: Ethics (transl. by S. Coit, 1932), vol. II, p. 70: „Just as the principle of motion need not itself be a motion, of life not itself life, just as the principles of knowledge are evidently far from being knowledge, so the universally ruling principle of the domain of value could very well be something else than a value." Cf. Toulmin, op. cit. 11 ff. on tests to recognise qualities which cannot be directly perceived. And cf. Urban, op. cit. 395—408 on the sufficient reason of valuation.

[210] „Substantiation" is a comprehensive notion denoting „verification" (used in relation to cognitive statements) as well as „justification" and „vindication" (used in relation to normative statements). The term „substantiation" seems to be more appropriate than „validation" as their common name because it aptly alludes to the process of seeking what is the axiotic ground (that is, the axiotic substance) of the existing valuations. On this problem cf. A. Sesonske: Cognitive and Normative, 1956, 17, Philosophy and Phenomenological Research, 1, at 12—15; H. Feigl: Validation and Vindication, in W. Sellars und J. Hospers (eds.), Readings in Ethical Theory, 1952, 667—680.

valid as correct, etc.[211]. There are two kinds of validity: objective and subjective. A valuation is objectively valid if it is substantiated by reference to criteria provided by *expressed* norms, for example, by written rules (statutory law, moral codes, etc.) or by norms manifested in the behaviour patterns of valuating subjects (customary law, rules of etiquette, etc.). A valuation is subjectively valid if it is substantiated by reference to criteria which exist only in the private givenness of the valuating subject, that is, they exist as criteria provided by the norms which the subject has never communicated to other intellects or which, if they have been communicated, have not obtained any lasting embodiment in signs enabling them to be ascertained later. Subjective validity is not identical with arbitrariness. A valuation is arbitrary if no pre-existing norm whatsoever can be indicated in accordance with which it has been performed. If a valuation is substantiable in accordance with a certain pre-existing norm, it is valid under this norm; if a valuation is not substantiable in accordance with a certain pre-existing norm, it is invalid under this norm. Arbitrary valuations may be substantiable in accordance with certain pre-existing norms, but in case of such valuations the valuating subject does not attempt at all to substantiate them by recourse to any normative principle. Substantiated valuations may be called „judgments“[212]. Arbitrary valuations may be called „mere prizings“. When an axiotic circumstance is constituted by an attribution of a value — valid, invalid, or arbitrary — to an object, a notion of this axiotic circumstance is formed by the intellect performing the act of attribution. This notion constitutes an individual axiotic standard corresponding to the respective axiotic circumstance. Thus an idea of truth, an idea of evil, and an idea of justice are axiotic standards. Where the intellect does not in-tend any *particular* axiotic circumstance but a *kind* of axiotic circumstance characterised by a value in the transsubjective sense, general axiotic standards are formed by the intellect. Axiotic standards (both individual and general) like valuations, can be valid, invalid, or arbitrary.

In order that the attribution of the metavalue „high“ and „low“ may be considered valid, there must be criteria[213] by reference to which a valuation of a value can be substantiated, and a value (in the objective sense) as an axiotic circumstance can be constituted which would be a basis for a valid axiotic standard. That such criteria are difficult to find is manifest from a great variety of viewpoints adopted in essentially the same valuations made even within well-integrated human communities. The lack of objective criteria of axiotic dignity gives rise to value-conflicts in everyday life, which has engendered

[211] The criteria in reference to which the validity of a valuation is determined constitute the substance of this validity; they subsist in relation to the *existing* acts of valuation.

[212] For a similar use of the term „judgment“ see Lewis, op. cit. 457.

[213] For an attempt to formulate rules providing criteria of axiotic dignity see F. Brentano: Vom Ursprung sittlicher Erkenntnis, 1921, 24 ff., 61 ff. Cf. Scheler, op. cit. 120–130.

the opinion that there are irremovable antinomies in the values themselves[214]. This however, does not affect the fact that values are apprehensible as organised in hierarchies. It appears, however, that a comprehensive hierarchy in which every value would find its place on the levels of axiotic dignity is nothing but an ideal. The extreme incommensurability of many entities to which values are attributed makes even a considerable approximation to such an ideal a vain hope. All that may be hoped for is apprehension of certain kinds of values, for example, moral values, organised in a hierarchy of axiotic levels[215].

Inquiries into the domain of values have proved difficult. All human passions operate in this domain, because values are experienced in the emotive acts of the mind: they are always involved when something is apprehended as the object of desire or aversion, love or hate, admiration or abhorrence. Since various human passions are involved in the experience of values, the inquirer is prone to see the domain of values in the light of his sympathies and antipathies, of his good and bad moods. It is common to expect to find more in the domain of values than actually is to be found there, and so subjective or arbitrary conceptions of perfection, absoluteness, and of other high ideals are projected into it. These projections yield pseudoanswers to many essential questionings of man, answers which tend to become a ground from which many ethical and political passions arise constituting enormous barriers for human communication. Thus there is a great danger that the inquirer of values will be locked in the enchanted circle of passions dimming and disturbing his axiotic „sight"[216]. Exploration of the domain of values has proved difficult also because of the obstacles that exist for a semantic approach to it[217]. In no language is there a sufficient selection of words signifying notions that denote values. Thus speaking of values on a scholarly level sometimes requires awkward circumscriptions, paranyms, and terminological innovations. This makes the interchange of thoughts difficult even for scholars, makes them often engage in merely verbal disputes where there is only an „appearance" of human communication but no „reality" of it. The veil of obscurity which enshrouds the problem of values appears largely to be due to man's shortcomings, and perhaps not at all to the ontological peculiarities of axiotic being[218].

---

[214] See G. Radbruch's report in Le But du Droit, 1938, 162: *„Pour ma part, je prétends qu'il y a antinomie non pas seulment dans le monde des faits, mais aussi dans le monde des idées."*

[215] For a limited hierarchy of values see R. Le Senne: Traité de Morale Générale, 1949, 678–681.

[216] Nevertheless „there is truth about values and, with respect to value in objects, a truth which can be missed". See Lewis, op. cit. 413. In this connection see also the discussion of Lewis on subjectivity and objectivity in reference to the cognition of values ibid. ch, xiii, esp. pp. 414 ff., 421 ff.

[217] Cf. A. Campbell Garnett: The Moral Nature of Man, 1952, 14, 115–131.

[218] Cf. N. Hartmann: Ethics (transl. by S. Coit, 1932), vol. III, p. 262: „Antinomies prove nothing against the coexistence of what is antinomically

12. The Axiological Aspect of Justice

To clarify the axiological aspect of justice, the main task appears to be to determine the relations between the just and other axiotic attributes. The rational penetration into the *designata* of the term „justice“ in all of its senses largely depends on the apprehension of these relations.

When determination of the relations of the just to other axiotic attributes is sought, it is to be noted that there can be no *values* logically sub- or superordinated to it. All values are eidetic individualities, and thus no value can be the *genus* of another value. The highest axiological *genus* of a value is „value“. „Value“ as a *genus* is no value itself; it is no eidetic individuality but an eidetic generality. Since the just is a value in the subjective sense, the special axiological *genus* of the just is *„axiotic attribute“*. Correspondingly, the special axiological *genus* of justness is „axiotic character“ and of justice (properly so called) — „axiotic circumstance“.

To find the *genus proximum* of the just, it is necessary to determine the *species* of the *genus* „value“ to which the just belongs. So it can be said, firstly, that the just is a positive value. This follows from the fact that in the value-type of the just there is the negative value „unjust“, standing at the opposite pole to the just, and the neutral value „neither-just-nor-unjust“, standing between the just and the unjust in the value-type in question. The status of the just as a positive value does not, of course, exclude the possibility of its having negative nature in relation to another supposedly higher value (perhaps, for example, in relation to the sacred, and the sublime). The proposition that the just is a positive value determines only its place in its value-type.

To continue the search of the *genus proximum* of the just, it can be said, secondly, that the just is a simple value. This determination may be contested on the ground that the just is frequently attributed to an entity to which also, for example, the good[219], the right[220], the true[221], or the beautiful[222] is attributed. This fact, however, does not establish that these values are component elements of the just. The noësis of the just may be associated with the noëses of these values, but can also be

---

divided, even though they should be proved genuine antinomies, that is, should be insoluble. They prove the inability of thought to comprehend the co-existence.“

219 See Cicero: De Officiis, 1, 7.

220 See E. Brunner: Gerechtigkeit, 1943, 27 ff.

221 For instance, Disraeli is reported to have said: „Justice is truth in action.“ See H. Potter: The Quest of Justice, 1951, 6.

222 Cf. the conception of Leibniz that the realisation of justice imports also aesthetic enjoyment *„comme une belle musique ou bien une bonne architecture contente les esprits bienfaits“*. Quoted by G. Radbruch: Rechtsphilosophie, 4th ed. 1950, 338. Cf. also J. Pieper: Über die Gerechtigkeit, 1953, 38.

dissociated from them. Even without, and even in opposition to, the experiencing of the good, the beautiful, etc., the just can be experienced and its corresponding noëmatic object constituted.

To determine the just further, it can be said, thirdly, that the just is an ethical value. Speaking of values in the subjective sense, ethical values are those axiotic attributes to which a conduct, that is, a voluntary behaviour[223] conforms; they are values attributed to the subject's commissions and omissions, doings and not-doings, provided that these acts have been *willed* by the subject. Such axiotic attributes are, for example, the charitable, the equitable, and the merciful[224]. As examples of the axiotic attributes which are not ethical values, the beautiful (an aesthetic value), the true (an epistemic value), and the correct (a logical value) may be mentioned. It is to be noted that ethical values are sometimes attributed to objects which do not appear to constitute conduct. Thus a legal order is valuated as just and a man is valuated as charitable. This fact, however, is no refutation of the qualification of the just as an ethical value. In some instances notions referring to ethical values are used paranymically. In other instances, voluntary behaviour is implied in the object of attribution but this implication is not obvious.

The final determination of the just in order to find its *genus proximum* can be made by saying that the just is a value to which the conduct that accords a subject its due conforms. Its due[225] is not necessarily accorded to a subject when its conduct is valuated as charitable. Charity may be done even when the subject has in no way deserved the charity; it may be a pure act of brotherly love, magnanimity, pity, forgiveness. The same holds for the equitable. To correct the hardship that the realisation of justice may entail *(dura lex sed lex)*, the individual needs of a particular case are taken into account and an equitable relief is given. Equity is a charity applied through legal channels[226]. Both the equitable and the charitable may, of course, rightly be attributed to the same object of attribution; thus justice may coincide with equity and charity. To accord benefits both out of brotherly love and to accord them out of conviction that the subject is given its due are not mutually exclusive. In the case of an equitable

---

[223] Cf. Pieper, op. cit. 41 ff. Cf. also Aristotle: Ethica Eudemia, V, 5, 17, 1134 a, 1–6; M. Hamburger: Morals and Law, 1951, 53.

[224] Man's involuntary acts do not appear to have conformity to these values, for example, his unconscious movements or his behaviour caused by a *vis maior*.

[225] The classical term for „one's (its) due" is *„suum"*.

[226] With this conception of equity cf. the Aristotelian view in Ethica Nicomachea, V, 10, 6, 1137 b, 26, that the nature of the equitable is a correction of law where it is defective owing to its universality. On the Aristotelian conception of equity see Hamburger, op. cit. 93–105. For the notion of equity as entertained by Continental legal philosophers see M. Rümelin: Die Billigkeit im Recht, 1921; J. Binder: Philosophie des Rechts, 1925, 396–409.

relief, the equitable is attributed to a behavior on the grounds of moral considerations competing with the criteria of justness provided by the law existing at a particular time and place[227]. Its due may be accorded to a subject also when an act which is lawful is performed with respect to this subject. A positive law is an elaborate set of norms providing what may largely constitute criteria of justness. What is deemed to have justness according to a positive law may not coincide with legal certainty under the same law[228]. Legal uncertainty is a defect of law, consequently also a defect of the respective criteria of justness. But legal uncertainty may give scope for higher considerations of justice than those embodied in the positive law, and call for the realisation of a more advanced justice than the one realisable under this law. Where law is uncertain, situations emerge which do not permit legal solutions of some cases to be given. Thus in relation to this law, attribution of the just to a conduct may not be validly performed, and this conduct is to be qualified, by reference to the criteria of justness provided by this law, as neither-just-nor-unjust.

With the above determinations of the axiotic attribute „just“ the stage is reached at which the *genus proximum* of the just may be formulated: The just is a positive simple ethical axiotic attribute to which the conduct that accords a subject its due conforms.

For the clarification of the axiological aspect of justice the other problem to be considered is the place of the just in the hierarchy of values. To determine this place it is necessary to discuss the relations of the just to other values with which it appears to have an affinity or to stand in tension. This affinity and tension of the just exists, first of all,

---

[227] Consider this situation in the development of the English law of equity. On English equity see W. Friedmann: Legal Theory, 1949, 342 ff. On the ethical nature of the principle of equity see A. Campbell Garnett: The Moral Nature of Man, 1952, 188—193. On equity see also P. Vinogradoff: Outlines of Historical Jurisprudence, 1920, 63—69; H. Cairns: Legal Philosophy from Plato to Hegel, 1947, 107—110.

[228] The problem of the relations between justice and legal certainty was the main theme of discussion at the Third Session of the International Institute of Legal Philosophy and Sociology in Rome in 1937. Radbruch advocated the view that there were genuine antinomies between justice, legal certainty, and common weal. These antinomies could not be limited only to the appearances but must exist even in the realm of ideas. See G. Radbruch: Le But du Droit, in Le But du Droit: Bien Commun, Justice, Sécurité, 1938, 48—59. Delos advocated the contrary view contending that there were no antinomies between these values but they were in harmony with each other. See J.-T. Delos: Le Buts du Droit, ibid. 29—47. To Radbruchs words: *„Je n'ai pas peur des antinomies irréconciliables: se décider c'est vivre“* (p. 162), Delos answered: *„Vivre ce ne pas décider entre des antinomies, mais c'est s'ouvrir à la verité et par là s'égaler a elle . . .“* (p. 163). On the problem of legal certainty in relation to justice see also E. García Maynez: Justice and Legal Security (transl. by A. Child, 1949), 3, Philosophy and Phenomenological Research, 496—509.

with the value „equitable“. Although equity in many cases appears rightly to override justice, the latter nevertheless appears rightly to prevail in many other cases. It prevails because high ethical considerations such as common weal and legal certainty make it preferable. Thus it cannot be said that the equitable has a higher axiotic dignity than the just. It appears that they are on an equal level in the hierarchy of values. The same appears to hold *mutatis mutandis* for the relation of the just to the charitable[229].

An essential affinity and tension of the just exists also with the values „good“, „true“, „correct“, „beautiful“, and „right“. In popular and semi-popular conceptions, justice tends to be identified with the axiotic circumstances corresponding to these axiotic attributes. With these conceptions insights may be contrasted which show that justice may very well coincide or be associated also with the opposite axiotic circumstances. The Latin adages *„summum ius summa iniuria“* and *„fiat iustitia pereat mundus“* indicate that what is deemed to have justness may be deemed also to have badness[230]. If it is considered that just decisions may be based on false evidence, on distortion of truth, and on logically faulty reasoning, something that is valuated as just may be judged as untrue[231] and incorrect. Since the same decisions can very well be based on untidy, tortuous, confused — consequently ugly — reasoning, there must be occasions when justice is associated with the opposite of beauty[232]. Of the above attributes, the just has perhaps the closest affinity with the right, because distributive justice is characterised by right proportion between the deserts and the benefits, and in synallagmatic justice equality of service and counterservice implies a right proportion[233]. However, it is nevertheless possible to valuate as just what is valuated as wrong, for instance, when justice is realised through acts in *fraudem legis*. In all these relations of tension, it is impossible to decide *a priori* whether justice should be sacrificed to truth, beauty, etc., or *vice versa*, on the mere grounds of the axiotic dignity of the values in question. It appears that the just, the good, the true, the correct, and the beautiful may have a claim of being axiologically placed only on an equal rank, and that conflicts between their corresponding axiotic circumstances must remain axiologically insoluble when in the particular cases of conflict there are no higher axiotic considerations to give prevalence to one of these values as against the others.

---

[229] On the distinction of the just and the charitable see L. Lavelle: Traité des Valeurs, 1955, vol. II, p. 29.

[230] See Radbruch: Rechtsphilosophie, pp. 95, 278. See also id.: Vorschule der Rechtsphilosophie, 1947, 23.

[231] Cf., however, the dictum of W. Fuchs: Neoklassik in der Rechtsphilosophie, 1954, 92: *„Dike et Aletheia filiae Jovis: ideo justitiam et veritatem sorores esse censemus. Sine veritate et prudentia justi esse non possumus.“*

[232] Cf. Potter, op. cit. 23.

[233] See Brunner, op. cit. 27 ff.

There are relations of affinity and tension of the just also with the useful and the expedient[234]. These values[235] are, however, evidently of a lower axiotic dignity than the just, and the conflict of justice with the axiotic circumstances corresponding to them ought always to be decided in favour of justice, unless they are supported by values of an axiotic dignity which is the same or higher than the axiotic dignity of the just.

Since the hierarchy of values is constituted by the attribution of the metavalues „high" and „low" to values, the place which belongs to the just on the levels of axiotic dignity depends on the principles by reference to which this attribution is performed. Thus fanatics in causes of justice such as those whose minds are deranged by paranoid ideas may consider the just to be of the highest axiotic dignity. A thoroughly practical man may accord to it a place somewhere below the useful. And he who has a rather perverse axiotic sense, may even place the just below the pleasurable. There are no *a priori* grounds to determine the place of the just in the hierarchy of values. When arbitrariness and mere subjectivity are sought to be transcended in answering the question, What is the place of the just in the hierarchy of values?, the answer has to be given by reference to certain objective criteria of axiotic dignity. If this question is sought to be answered by reference to general ethical convictions crystallised in Western civilisation, these criteria indicate that the just does not occupy the place of the *Summum Bonum*. But it is on a plane not far from the apex of the hierarchy of values. Above the just there are usually placed religious values such as the sublime, the sacred, and the holy. The just occupies a place immediately, or almost immediately[236], below them on the same level with the charitable, the equitable, the true, the correct, the beautiful, and the right.

Fourth Discourse

Having concluded the central part of my inquiry, which dealt with the analysis of justice, I now feel I should pause and think of what I have attained. My attention, no longer absorbed in philosophical details, roams over the whole field covered, and encounters there a number of matters which make me feel uneasy. Various doubts invade my mind, and I fear that my enterprise has fallen short in many respects.

Although at the very outset of my venture I reconciled myself to the inevitability of entering into circuitous reasoning, I nevertheless

---

[234] On the relations of the just with the useful and the expedient see C. K. Allen: Justice and Expediency, in P. Sayre (ed.): Interpretations of Modern Legal Philosophies, 1947, 15–28, esp. at 21–28. Cf. Bentham: Principles of Morals and Legislation, ch. x, s. xl; Spencer: Justice, ch. vii; Hume: An Inquiry concerning the Principles of Morals, s. iii („Of Justice").

[235] On the nature of these values see N. Hartmann: Ethik, 3rd ed. 1949, 88; G. Moore: Principia Ethica, 1929, 169.

[236] It may be contended that in the ethical convictions as crystallised in Western civilisation, certain high moral values such as the magnanimous and the charitable have an axiotic dignity higher than that of the just.

feel alarmed at the thought that I actually did enter into it. Most conspicuously this happened when I tried to describe the ontological categories. But was there any alternative? It seems that to attempt to escape from *circullus vitiosus* is of no avail at least in ontological reasoning. When circling thoughts in fundamental philosophical efforts are diverted from their movement, they tend to take a tangential course and begin *regressus in infinitum*. To reach the ultimate ground on which the mind can stand appears to be hopeless in philosophy. The best we may expect here is perhaps that the mind will learn to soar in the *ápeiron*, so that thought can steadily move towards the receding and widening horizons[237] of the All. Philosophical grounds appear themselves to be groundless; they are not absolutely firm, not something on which an inquiring mind could find a final resting place. This seems to be somehow good. Philosophy thus is a perpetual dissolvent of the ontic enduring into which science, religion, arts, and other concerns of the mind tend to head, and so it keeps us in touch with reality, the essence of which is not Enduring but Becoming. Philosophy does not offer positions for standing but points for understanding[238]. Being in an infinite regress, thought may be able to come to points, above the reach of practical or scientific reasoning, from which we can „see" entities in a more favourable perspective and thus come into a better „acquaintance" with them[239]. A circuitous statement may have at least the merit of saying the same thing in other words. And these other words may be, in particular cases, better vehicles to convey the intuitions of the entities meant than are the words initially employed[240].

Thinking of my ontological inquiries into justice, it disquiets me that I have employed certain terms inconsistently with my purposes. Almost all the terms by which I have attempted to signify the notions of categories convey spatial-temporal intuitions; but the notions of the realm of eidetic being — to which categories belong — are intended to refer to non-spatial and non-temporal matters. And even at this very moment, addressing the problem of eidetic being, I was using expressions of the same nature, because „a realm" and „a matter" are, by the original intuitions of the words, ontic entities. My division of eidetic being into inherent, adherent, and extraherent being employed words of ontic

[237] On the philosophical concept of horizon see H. Kuhn: The Phenomenological Concept of Horizon, in M. Farber (ed.): Philosophical Essays in Memory of Edmund Husserl, 1940, 106–123.

[238] Cf. M. Heidegger: Sein und Zeit, 7th ed. 1953, 8, 152 ff.; S. E. Toulmin: The Place of Reason in Ethics, 1950, 130.

[239] On the problem of direct experience see B. Russell: An Inquiry into Meaning and Truth, 3rd impr. 1948, 236–246.

[240] In scientific thought *circulus vitiosus* and *regressus in infinitum* are, of course, as far as possible to be avoided. This is because the existing order of scientific knowledge makes such resorts unnecessary. If they are nevertheless employed, the scholar is not taking full advantage of the existing system of scientific knowledge, or the particular science has not yet achieved the level of a systematic knowledge.

intuitions throughout. And even now, using the word „division", I seem to be moving on the ontic plane. For this qualm I have the following remedy: With an *ignoratio elenchi* I say that I am not guilty because others who have struggled with the same philosophical problems have been guilty of the same failure. And further I can say that a full set of ontological expressions free from ontic intuitions for signifying notions of eidetic entities is not available in conventional language. To create and to employ new words altogether for this purpose would separate my thought from the tradition of philosophical expression and thus gravely affect its communicability. The situation of philosophical nomenclature is quite different from that of, for example, chemistry where even verbal monstrosities created by the inventors of new drugs are unblushingly used. The pressure of practical needs causes men engaged in the fields like chemistry to learn, in addition to other things they ought to know, the novel names that have been created to designate new items of scientific knowledge. In philosophy, however, the new does not have such a significance as in science and there is no considerable pressure of practical needs to learn about philosophical matters. The main motivating force of philosophical inquiries is perhaps still the love for wisdom; and this love may shrink back from creations that are too strange, too new. Philosophers have habitually employed metaphorical expressions[241]. The majority of ontological terms are metaphors. To be able to think in these tropes, it is necessary to invalidate *a limine* their direct reference and to be prepared to find that through them something quite different is meant than what is shown by their original intuitions.

Concerning my epistemological inquiries, I am afraid that I was not able to show sufficiently the ways for achieving distinct, clear, and true knowledge of justice. And I am afraid that I was not able to show sufficiently the reasons why my propositions relating to justice are true rather than false. Here I can ease my conscience with the consideration that the function of philosophy can hardly be conceived as that of diclosing absolute truth[242]. Moreover I have declared the scope of my work to be limited. I proposed only to present a sketch of the fundamental principles of justice. The purpose I had in view for this sketch was not to prove them definitely, not to elaborate them finally, but to indicate ways for their apprehension. It seems to me that the apprehension of the fundamental principles of an entity such as justice is something which no inquirer can *supply* to others. All he can do is to lead those who are engaged in the same or in an essentially similar

---

[241] Cf. K. Jaspers: Von der Wahrheit, 1947, 398 ff.; P. Tillich: Love, Power, and Justice, 1954, 37; Toulmin, op. cit. 44 ff.

[242] Cf. G. Santayana: The Realm of Essence, 1928, xiii: „The absolute truth has its own intangible reality and scorns to be known. The function of mind is rather to increase the wealth of the universe in the spiritual dimension, by adding appearance to substance and passion to necessity, and by creating private perspectives, and those emotions of wonder, adventure, curiosity and laughter which omniscience would exclude."

cognitive enterprise to conditions of the intellect from which they can each for themselves perform the acts of apprehension. The *apprehenda* of these acts may appear to be like configurations that can be found in a cloud, in which everyone as an isolated perceiver is likely to see different shapes and shadings, but would see essentially the same things if methods are described and expectations created to see particular entities at a particular part of the cloud. The common *ad-prehensio* of the configurations may be sufficient for a common orientation about the cloud whose „unstructured“ constitution is compatible with many structures „found“ in it by apprehending minds[243].

About my logical inquiries into justice, strangely, I do not seem to entertain any serious doubts. I do feel a certain disquietude about some terminological matters such as my specific use of the word „statement“ and about my rather individual treatment of the problem of interrogatives, imperatives, optatives, and putatives. But these appear to be incidental matters. My feeling sure about my logical inquiries makes me suspicious that I might have fallen here into dogmatism, which makes me doubt about the consistency of my thinking that I designed to be something open, something always subject to doubt. The spearhead of this qualm I can avert with the consideration that to be skeptical about logical principles appears to be something out of place. There may be incidental doubts about logical matters affecting different side issues, and there may be an encompassing vague doubt about the whole of logic, but as a formal discipline of the principles according to which a correct reasoning ought to occur, logic seems to stand beyond skepsis. It is the framework even of the propositions asserting skeptical views. Formal logic is the branch of philosophy which, from its ancient beginnings, has remained relatively well settled. Certainly, its scope has been extended, some of its tools have been made keener, and approaches to its problems have varied, but its pillars have remained intact. The principles of formal logic are evident to a very high degree. It is useless to entertain theoretical doubts about them unless they prove unreliable in the practical experience of those who employ them. Until reasons which permit such unreliability to be asserted[244] are forthcoming, a thinker may rest in a „dogmatic slumber“ on the traditional pillars of logic.

My axiological inquiries into justice disquiet me with the impasse in which they seem to have ended. I was unable to indicate anything

---

[243] Cf. W. Van Orman Quine: From a Logical Point of View, 1953, 19, who discussing the problem of ontology comes to the conclusion: „ . . . the question what ontology actually to adopt still stands open, and the obvious councel is tolerance and experimental spirit.“

[244] The logical paradoxes are an important theoretical subject of study but they are seldom of great practical significance. On the problem of logical paradoxes see generally C. I. Lewis and C. H. Langford: Symbolic Logic, 1932, 438–485; K. J. J. Hintikka: Identity, Variables, and Impredicative Definitions, 1956, 21, Journal of Symbolic Logic, 225–245. See also the forthcoming sequel of this article entitled „Vicious Circle Principle and the Paradoxes“ in the same periodical.

solid to support my conceptions of values, criteria of validity, and the place of justice among other values. Is there not indeed the Right Reason enthroning over the plurality of conflicting value judgments, a criterion which would make it possible to decide any axiotic conflict and enable us to find a cogent answer to the question, What to prefer?, at any time when a problem of preference arises? Perhaps there is this Right Reason, but I am sure I do not posses it, and I do not know to what degree I participate in it. When other people say that they have true knowledge of the Right Reason, how can I test the truth of their assertion? And if there should be a privileged one who has this knowledge, how can others share this knowledge, and how can they know that someone has this knowledge? So it seems to me that I need not be concerned about the inconclusiveness of my axiological inquiries. It belongs to the situation of man's dwelling in the world that much that is of transcending importance for him is obscure to him. Where in valuational problems clear and objective principles are not available for us we just have to rely on our own subjective sense of the right or the wrong supported merely by an axiotic intuition which operates only in concrete situations and may be incapable of generalisation.

I seem to have reasoned myself out of my immediate philosophical qualms, but there are others on the threshold of my consciousness. The feeling of uneasiness with which I commenced my present discourse is still with me. I find it useless to reflect on my philosophical problems and argue about them any further now. But I am interested to know, what these other matters which still disturb me are; and to take notice of them, I propose simply to observe the contents of my mind, to have a passive awareness of them. Taking this notice I become aware of a gloom. I feel sorry about something. My attention turned to this something, I have the impression that I have built all my work on sand and that there is no rock visible on which I could start building anew. I also have the impression that my attempts to reassure myself with the above considerations in the present discourse are self-deceptions. These impressions suddenly turn into a qualm about the expressions by which I have tried to clarify the fundamental principles of justice. I feel that at places I have spoken with too much conviction and that often I have used words and phrases which are too inadequate or misleading, being novel or clumsy or violating customs of speech. But a moment later I notice that I feel a regret for having tried to make everything transparent in my essay. Having refused the protection of obscurity, I have exposed my intellectual limitations in all their nakedness. Having attained no assured insights which would satisfy me, I have only confused issues and achieved humiliation. This humiliation does not give me any pleasure as some sufferings may give to those who are able to perceive the depths and beauty of the painful[245]. Even the thought that through philosophy we

[245] On the significance of the experience of the painful for man's intellectual pursuits see Th. Reik: Masochism in Modern Man (transl. by M. H. Beigel and G. M. Kurth, 2nd impr. 1949), 367–433.

learn humility does not comfort me; this rather makes me despair about my whole philosophical enterprise, and about the whole of philosophy. And now I notice that I have ended in despair.

From this despair there seems to be no outlet through my intellectual efforts. I feel I am a prisoner of my own thoughts constituting an impenetrable wall of obscurity around me. I had better even give up the search for deliverance and light. It seems to give me some relief just to observe my fleeting gloomy thoughts without making any effort to find an expression for them. But it gives me even a better relief to turn my glance outwards to the night sky, the ferries gliding over the harbour, and the dark waters on which they move and on which numerous lights reflect. I have discontinued my concern with the principles of justice, to resume it some other time, but not today.

Fifth Discourse

All day I have suffered from a nameless anxiety. It has shifted from object to object without being able to shape itself into a definite fear. This floating anxiety has attached itself to my sundry trivial daily affairs, to the conditions of my body, and to various contents of my mind. But with any of these objects it has stayed only for a short while, soon continuing its drift. In this floating anxiety I feel desolate, and this desolation is uncanny. My anxiety may be an aftereffect of the despair in which my reflections ended last night. But what is its escaping content? About what is my anxiety anxious?

Trying to fathom the reason and content of my anxiety[246], I come to think that I still have not managed to resolve the uneasiness I have felt about the present inquiry. It is possible that the nameless anxiety from which I have suffered today springs from a fear that my efforts might prove futile. Unprepared to carry this fear in my consciousness, I seem to transfer the anxiety about my work to other objects; but on these it won't remain fixed. To fight my floating anxiety I must try to master my original anxiety by withdrawing its ground. This I could hope to do if I were able to show what aims I still can pursue by my further inquiry. So far I have obtained a preconceptual notion of justice from the heuristic data of its various current conceptions. This notion I then tried to raise to a rational level by considering its various philosophical aspects. It should be possible now to base a concept of justice on these preparatory considerations. For this purpose the definitions of justice, justness, the just, and the idea of justice are to be formulated. This will be my immediate task, and about its outcome I should not be apprehensive. I have analysed and delimited justice in its various senses already in a number of propositions, and it should not be difficult to integrate them into corresponding definitions.

My next task is to deal with the problem of the criteria of justness. Without a demonstration of these criteria, our knowledge of justice would

---

[246] On the significance of anxiety for the philosophical approach to reality see L. Lavelle: Le Moi et Son Destin, 1936, 65–117, esp. p. 77.

be of little value, since valid attributions of the just can be distinguished from its invalid attributions only by reference to criteria of justness. About this matter I have more reason to be apprehensive. The proper end of a treatment of the criteria of justness seems to be a set of principles transcending my subjectivity. But this transcending seems to be a hopeless enterprise. It appears to be impossible to escape from the enclosure of my subjectivity whatever I may do in or with my thoughts[247]. The attainment of transsubjective criteria of validity would still be a feat of my subjectivity. But if it is necessarily so, why should I be concerned? Let the transsubjectivity I am striving for be my subjectivity then, as long as it is not a *mere* subjectivity of my own, but one which I can share with other subjects, one which can be intersubjectivity[248]. I am sure that there is such subjectivity, a subjectivity which is not my capriciousness, not existing in ephemeral states of my passing moods, but constituted through persistent lengthy comprehensive efforts of my mind to escape from its isolation. My mere subjectivity I can transcend through extensive circumspective reasoning, through radical doubt, and through efforts to communicate[249].

To escape from „mere subjectivity" thus appears to be possible to me. To transcend this subjectivity I have to find my authentic Self, and to engage it in all my efforts about myself and about others. This authentic Self does not appear, however, to be something simply to be resorted to, even not to be unearthed, recovered. It does not seem to exist as an actuality at all but only as a possibility[250] that is never completely actualisable. Since the authentic Self means no „thing" for me but only a possible state of my existence, which state is a *limes*, a noumenon, an *ek-stasis*[251], I try to apprehend this Self as a lasting projection and to „see" this projection with the greatest possible clarity so that its notion could be an effective regulative idea for my actions. I learn to perform this projection in communication of my phenomenal

---

[247] Cf. C. I. Lewis: Analysis of Knowledge and Valuation, 1946, 263: „All knowledge is knowledge of someone; and ultimately no one can have any ground for his beliefs which does not lie within his own experience."

[248] On the intersubjectivity of value-findings see Lewis, op. cit. 423, who uses the term „community" for what is termed „intersubjectivity" in the present inquiry. According to Lewis, the dichotomy „subjective-objective (including reference to community or idiosyncracy)" should not be confused with the dichotomy „veridical-illusory".

[249] On the problem of human communication see K. Jaspers: Philosophie, 2nd ed. 1948, 338—396; id.: Einführung in die Philosophie, 1950, 9 ff., 33, 36; J. Stone: Legal Controls of International Conflict, 1954, xli—xliii.

[250] Cf. R. Polin: Against Wisdom, 1955, 16, Philosophy and Phenomenological Research 1, at 16: „We cannot speak of a human nature as something given once for all but of a human nature growing truly in an unforeseeable becoming."

[251] Cf. G. Marcel: Being and Having, 1951, 106: „It may be of my essence to be able to be not what I am"; L. Lavelle: De l'Etre, 2nd ed. 1947, 125; G. Allport: Becoming, 1955, 19: „Personality is less a finished product than a transitive process" and p. 61: „The proprium is not a thing . . ."

Self with other phenomenal Selves[252], in which occurrence the experience of achievements and failures to lead a fuller mental life are shared[253].

Communication and the apprehension of the noumenal Self are problems bordering the field of psychology, because their investigation requires consideration of empirical realities in which the human mind is actually participating. To apprehend the noumenal Self as the authentic Self, the principal ways in which man behaves inauthentically should be pointed out. The modes of inauthenticity are fundamental barriers of human communication; they are also obstacles for the apprehension and realisation of justice. Separated from each other by these barriers, men cannot be expected to be just[254]: in the isolation of their „mere subjectivity" they are prone to arbitrary valuations[255]. Thus psychological problems of justice appear to confront me as a theme to be discussed. However, my duty to perform this task is only secondary. For an inquiry into the *fundamental* principles of justice, to enter upon the field of an empirical science such as psychology is to digress. Therefore its barest outlines will be sufficient for the present essay. I have no reason to fear that I shall not be able to draw these outlines.

I seem to have come to an end of the discussion of my anxiety about the present inquiry: I thought that I was afraid of its failing to achieve anything worthwhile, but now I feel that there is little reason to entertain this fear. Nevertheless the nameless anxiety from which I have suffered all day still seizes me. And I have not found anything that may constitute a real object of fear. About what then is my anxiety anxious[256]? Can it be that it is anxious of nothing? But then, what is this nothing? My firm ontological belief is that nothing as *no entity* is inconceivable. It can mean only *no thing,* that is to say, nothing concrete, nothing here and now; which is still something, must have some kind of being, even though this being may be phrased „non-being". The nothing about which my anxiety is anxious thus appears to be the infinity of unknown possibilities into which I am in danger of slipping if I drift aimlessly in my life, trying endlessly ot analyse everything, radically doubt everything, hoping that at some time somewhere by someone cogent insights will be gained and questions irrefutably answered. The nothing as the object of my anxiety must haunt me if I am without a pilot in my drifting thoughts, without authentic Self, without true faith. All my hopes ever to arrive somewhere, to have a rest at something, and to become authentic must

---

252 Cf. W. Percy: Symbol as Hermeneutic in Existentialism, 1956, 16, Philosophy and Phenomenological Research, 522, at 528: „The Thou is at once the source of my consciousness, the companion and co-celebrant of my discovery of being — and the sole threat to my unauthentic constitution of myself."

253 With the notion of the authentic Self cf. Jaspers' notion of *Existenz* in K. Jaspers: Von der Wahrheit, 1947, 76.

254 Cf. St. Thomas Aquinas' dictum in his *Ethicorum Aristotelis ad Nicomachum Expositio,* 8, 9, No. 1658: *„Sed justitia consistit in communicatione."*

255 See L. Lavelle: De l'Intimité Spirituelle, 1955, 115.

256 For a philosophical analysis of the problem of anxiety see M. Heidegger: Sein und Zeit, 7th ed. 1953, 184—191.

sink into the groundlessness of the infinity of possibilities if I do not have a faith which would give me some, even though temporary hold. But in what can I have faith, of what can I be certain? I am certain that I exist, however, from the mere statement: „*Ego sum sive existo*" nothing follows to support me in my anxiety and despair. Together with my existence, the statement asserts the frailty of my existence, reminding me of the inexorable fact that one day, if I continue to exist at all, I shall not be such as I am now; in other words, I shall die. But what support can I expect from my death? It is nothing else for me than a totality of indeterminate possibilities; the thought of it does not comfort me but frightens me: it is a comparatively static state of my anxious mind. Perhaps the only good it does for me is that it frightens me as a mirror reflecting my limited but transcendable phenomenal Self and thus makes me aware of the need actually to transcend it by becoming authentic as far as it lies in my power. Death is a limit-situation[257], a situation which is ultimate for my phenomenal Self; it is a situation from which I know there is „no exit" for me. Thoughts of it cause me to feel as though at the edge of doom, and make me see as something valuable everything that takes me away from the threatening doom. But am I authentic if I try to escape death under all circumstances? Are there not values of such axiotic dignity that for their sake it would be right to choose death rather than to escape it? I feel that there are such values, and that death is not the Supreme Evil.

Death is not the only limit-situation that confronts me; it is not the only threat that makes me anxious. Anxiety itself is a limit-situation. It is somehow always with my phenomenal Self if I am not forgetful of the fact that it fails, falls short. Just as I can make my own Self an object of my various concerns my anxiety, too, can become such an object. Thus I can be anxious about my anxiety. The uncanniness of my nameless anxiety from which I have suffered today now seems to me due to the premonition that my anxiety may become a boundless anxiety[258] an anxiety, which I have not yet experienced, but which I fear may overcome and overwhelm me. Such boundless anxiety I can surmise, and I apprehend as its noëmatic object the *Summum Malum*. Being the ultimate phase of a limit-situation, there is no beyond it for me. But even for my phenomenal Self there is an away from it, and this away is in the direction of love[259]. The contrast of anxiety[260] is love, the contrast of nameless anxiety is nameless love, the contrast of boundless anxiety is boundless love.

I know that I am capable of loving to some extent and to some degree. On rare occassions I have experienced love, as I have experienced anxiety, even without any definite object; that is, I have experienced a nameless

---

[257] On the notion of limit-situations see Jaspers: Philosophie, 467–512.

[258] Cf. P. Tillich: The Courage to Be, 2nd impr. 1953, 13.

[259] Cf. ibid. 23 ff.

[260] On the ontology of anxiety and on the relations of anxiety to fear, emptiness, meaninglessnes, and despair see ibid. ch. ii, esp. pp. 36–39, 46–51, 54–57.

love. But boundless love has never been an actual experience to me[261]. I can only vaguely surmise this ultimate love and so apprehend in the neighbourhood of its noëma the *Summum Bonum*. My actual experiences of love appear to me the base from which I can reach towards boundless love, if I somehow refine, expand, and enrich the emotion of love I know.

The reflection on boundless love and boundless anxiety confronts me with metaphysical problems. The noëmata of these emotions are the apex and counterapex of the hierarchies of values, in the proximity of which lie the levels of axiotic dignity and indignity of the just and the unjust. Thus my inquiry into the fundamentals of justice brings me also to the precincts of metaphysics. With an excursus into it, I propose to conclude the chapters of my essay.

VI. Concluding Considerations

13. The Concepts of Justice

To obtain concepts of justice, the various notions of justice distinguished and clarified in the foregoing considerations of the present inquiry are to be defined. These considerations suggest the following definition of justice (properly so called):

(1) Justice is the axiotic circumstance constituted by the attribution of the just to a social situation

Concerning this definition the following comments may be made: That „social[262] situation" is a determinant of the concept of justice, is a convention proposed by the definer of this concept; it is a matter established *per definitionem*[263]. „Justice" can be defined also in a different content, for example, perhaps so that its denotation covers the notion of justice signified in the phrases such as „Mr. Justice X" or „to complain with justice", but there appears to be no compelling reason for this choice. The element „social" in the determinant „social situation" indicates that a situation pertains to a plurality of interacting subjects[264] whose conduct is manifested outwardly. An outward manifestation of a conduct is that aspect or phase of a conduct which a person who is not the subject of the conduct can perceive through the senses. Since „axiotic circumstance" is equivalent to „value in the objective sense", „justice" can also be styled as „situational value"[265].

---

[261] The metaphysical idea of boundless love invites man neither to acquiesce in the actualities of the evil nor into repose of contemplation. It is rather a principle of a „loving struggle".

[262] For a definition of „social" cf. J. Dewey: Theory of Valuation, 1939, 10 ff., according to whom „social" means that „there is a form of behaviour of the nature of interaction and transaction between two or more persons".

[263] Cf. the statement of the conventionalistic conception of the definition by F. Kaufmann: Methodenlehre der Sozialwissenschaften, 1936, 32 ff., 48.

[264] Cf. J. Pieper: Über die Gerechtigkeit, 1953, 29 ff., 57.

[265] Cf. N. Hartmann: Ethik, 3rd ed. 1949, 424, who styles justice as *„Sachverhaltswert"*.

On the basis of the considerations in the previous course of the present inquiry, justness can be defined as follows:

(2) Justness is the axiotic character corresponding to the just

Concerning this definition the following comments may be made: Justness can be a character of a situation, of a person, of a law, etc., but it is so only because a conduct (actual or contemplated) that is deemed to have justness is an inherent quality of this situation, this person, this law, etc. In other words, the entity to which justness directly adheres is a conduct. Considering that justness is an eidetic individuality, it appears that it cannot be completely defined by classificatory methods[266]. This is so because narrowing the classes under which its concept would fall leads only to further classes, but never to individual concepts. The defining of eidetic as well as ontic individualities requires ostensive references, and their definitions are, in certain respect, ostensive definitions[267]. The ostensive references determine, even though in a general manner, the area of the „experiencing" referring to the individuality. Or, in other words, they direct the intellect to the noësis in which the individuality in question is intuited as a noëma[268]. In the definition of justness, the component „constituted by the attribution of the just" appears to be an ostensive reference.

On the basis of the considerations in the previous course of the present inquiry, the just can be defined as follows:

(3) The just is the positive simple ethical axiotic attribute to which the conduct that accords a subject its due in obligative-pretensive relations conforms

Concerning this definition the following comments may be made: The *„significatum"* „its" used in connection with the *„significatum"* „subject" in this definition indicates that, for the purposes of the apprehension of the just, any subject whatsoever will suffice insofar as such subject accords something to someone. For these purposes it is irrelevant whether this subject is a human being, a transcendent entity, or a legal construct. Such a wide denotation of „subject" is required to

---

[266] Like ontic individualities such as „Sokrates" or „this pen of mine" cannot completely be so defined.

[267] On ostensive definitions see B. Russell: Human Knowledge, 1948, 78—86; L. Wittgenstein: Philosophical Investigations (transl. by G. E. M. Anscomb, 1953), 4 ff., and Part I, passim. On ostension as applied to „teaching" simple qualities see S. E. Toulmin: The Place of Reason in Ethics, 1950, 16: „Simple qualities are taught ‚ostensively', i. e. by pointing out or instancing . . . objects having the quality"; cf. W. Van Orman Quine: From a Logical Point of View, 1953, 64—79, especially at 74—79. See also A.-T. Kliimann: Õiguskord, 1939, 65—89, who in this book (Legal Order) written in the Estonian language employs ostensive references for defining the concept „legal order".

[268] Cf. J. Stone: Legal Controls of International Conflict, 1954, 53 ff.

bring various ideas of justice under a common denominator. The subjects with which law and morality are mostly concerned are, of course, men. The same considerations hold, *mutatis mutandis,* for „accords" as employed in the above definition. The wide denotation of „accords" covers both „gives" and „withholds"[269].

As an element of the concept of the just, „due" connotes something that ought to belong to someone[270]. This entity is, however, not anything definite or certain. Therefore „due" may be said to be an indeterminate reference[271]. Rendering it determinate requires recourse to principles provided by certain norms. In seeking a more precise sense to „due" as relevant to determining „the just", the following principle may be considered: a due is accorded if equal benefits are accorded to equal subjects and unequal benefits to unequal subjects in right proportion[272]. The right proportion exists, however, if the subject deserving more obtains a greater benefit according to its deserts, and the subject deserving less obtains a lesser benefit according to his deserts. It is obvious that the indeterminacy of the reference „due" cannot be removed in this way, because the above propositions contain other indeterminate references. These references relegate in turn one to criteria by recourse to which one could decide when subjects are equal and when unequal, what benefits are equal and what unequal, and what is the measure of the deserts of the subjects so that right proportions would be constituted. The indeterminacy of the reference „due" can also not be removed by indicating that „due", as relevant to determining „the just", alludes to an order on which it is founded[273]. „Order", like „equality", is an indeterminate reference. Nevertheless, „due", „equality", and „order" are not unimportant for the determination of the concept of the just. There is a striving for one's due (as there are strivings for equality and order) almost universally present in mature human minds, even though what this due (or this equality or this order) that people are yearning and striving for precisely is may be obscure to them. The mentioning of „due", „equality", and „order" in connection with the just, therefore, somehow circumscribes the noësis (the experiencing) by which the just is intuitively apprehended as its noëma (as that which is or

[269] Cf. E. Wolf: Das Problem der Naturrechtslehre, 1955, 88.

[270] Cf. E. Brunner: Gerechtigkeit, 1943, 20—23, esp. p. 22; *„In diesem ‚gehört' steckt das ganze Pathos der Gerechtigkeit."* Cf. also Pieper, op. cit. 11—28.

[271] On the concept of „indeterminate reference" see J. Stone: The Province and Function of Law, 2nd ed. 1950, 185 ff. On the problem of the indeterminate in justice see E. N. Garlan: Legal Realism and Justice, 1941, 54—74; H. Kelsen: What Is Justice? 1957, 13—18.

[272] On the relations between equality and justice cf. H. Nef: Gerechtigkeit und Gleichheit, 1941, passim; W. D. Lamont: Principles of Moral Judgment, 1946, 134—148; A. Ross: Towards a Realistic Jurisprudence, 1946, 145.

[273] For a view that „order" is an essential of „justice" see Brunner, op. cit. 19—22.

is to be experienced by the experiencing). „Due“, „equality“, and „order“ thus are relevant to the determination of the just as ostensive references.

A further ostensive reference in the above definition of the notion of the just is „obligative-pretensive relations“[274]. This reference indicates that the experience in which the noëma „the just“ is apprehended occurs in conjunction with the noësis of the relations consisting in the circumstances that to a duty (obligation) corresponds a claim (a right, a pretension). Such relations are bilateral or synallagmatic[275]. „Duty“ in its wide sense designates the circumstance that a subject ought to do or ought not to do something (for example, to love his neighbour, to pay his debt, to abstain from fraud). „Claim“ in its wide sense designates the circumstance that a subject considers another subject to have the duty to do a duty or that there is an objective norm which attributes to the subject this considering[276]. Claims are thus founded on duties but not always on objective ones: in the subjective sense a claim exists when there is merely a subjective considering that there is a duty to do a duty. There are relations between the subjects where no claim corresponds to a duty. Thus if someone considers that he has a

---

[274] Cf. B. N. Cardozo: The Paradoxes of Legal Science, 2nd impr. 1930, 44. On the obligative-pretensive relations in general see I. Tammelo: Untersuchungen zum Wesen der Rechtsnorm, 1947, 79—81; 89 ff. Cf. A. Reinach: Zur Phänomenologie des Rechts, 1953, 21—86. For an analysis of right-duty relationship cf. also H. L. A. Hart: Are there Natural Rights? 1955, 64, Philosophical Review, 175, at 177—182.

The obligative-pretensive relation can be analysed into the following components: duty, claim, conduct, duty-subject, claim-subject, and considering (or attribution). Of these components conduct, duty-subject, claim-subject, and also the obligative-pretensive relation as a whole, seem to conform to the just. The object to which justness directly adheres is, however, conduct. A duty-subject, a claim-subject, or an obligative-pretensive relation may be deemed to have justness if the respective obligated or claimed conduct is deemed to have justness. Neither the obligated and the claimed conduct nor the obligative-pretensive relation need to be actual conduct or an actual relation. Thus we may speak of justness and of justice also with respect to possible conduct and relations, for instance when we expect that something should be just or we contend that something would be just *de lege feranda*.

[275] On the bilaterality of justice see G. Del Vecchio: Justice (ed. by A. H. Campbell, 1952), 83.

[276] Legal relations are obligative-pretensive relations *par excellence*. Apart from these, there are also obligative-pretensive religious and moral relations. Thus man may be regarded as having duties towards God, and God may be regarded as having claims with respect to these duties; and thus, from religious points of view man can be considered just or unjust according to how he behaves with respect to these duties and claims. Even God may be regarded as having duties and man corresponding claims, and thus God may be praised as being just. Of the moral relations, for example, telling the truth may be conceived as an obligative-pretensive relation: there is a moral duty to be truthful (if higher moral considerations do not forbid it), and there is a corresponding claim to this duty.

moral duty to perform an act of charity, there may be no one who considers him to have the duty to do this ostensible duty. Or, if there is an objective moral duty to love one's neighbour as one loves oneself, there may be nobody who considers an utterly unworthy person to have a claim to this love. The relations of this kind do not conform to the just: if a man is in need of charity and he is given no help, the withholding of charity may be valuated as bad, as unfair, as callous, but not as unjust; if one's neighbour is under certain circumstances not loved as one loves oneself, this may be considered as falling short of high religious ideals but not as unjust under human standards of justice[277].

On the basis of the considerations in the previous course of the present inquiry, the idea of justice can be defined as follows:

(4) The idea of justice is the axiotic standard which exists as a subject's notion of justice

There appears to be no need to make comments on this definition, since all components of its *definiens* should have been sufficiently clarified in the foregoing chapters of the present study.

All the above definitions are necessarily obscure as isolated propositions. They are expected to convey the intended *designata* on the basis of almost the whole of the present inquiry. The classical warning „*omnis definitio in iure civili periculosa est*"[278] applies to the definitions of justice insofar as one expects to see in them formulae which are enlightening *per se*. An isolated definition is a ground onto which one's expectations, prejudices, and ignorance are readily projected. It is apperceived differently when it is approached in serenity, in affection, or in annoyance. „*Omnis definitio periculosa*" contains also a proper warning for those who want to regard the definitions of justice as something final. With definitions like those of justice, the possibility of their revision must be left open as must further penetration into the problems they raise and elaboration of a fuller set of subdefinitions. The definitions of justice are, however, not dangerous if they are regarded as a convenient base departing from which their various implications: both their premisses and their corollaries, can be investigated and departing from which, if necessary, better formulations of the definitions or new definitions altogether can be sought[279].

---

277 On the relation between divine law and justice see Brunner, op. cit. 54–64.

278 See the dictum of Iavolenus in D. 50, 17, 202: „*Omnis definitio in iure civili periculosa est: parum est enim, ut non subverti posset.*" On the problem of the definition in law see H. L. A. Hart: Definition and Theory in Jurisprudence, 1954, 70, Law Quarterly Review, 37–60. On the difficulties and dangers in defining (especially in relation to legal terms) see S. I. Shuman: Jurisprudence and the Analysis of Fundamental Legal Terms, 1956, 8, Journal of Legal Education, 437–467, at 439–443.

279 Cf. Benjamin N. Cardozo's remarks on the related matter in Cardozo, op. cit. 35 ff.

14. The Criteria of Justness and the Arbiters of Justice

The criteria of justness are the principles by reference to which the validity of attribution of the just is ascertained[280]. Like all validity criteria, they are either subjective or objective. Valuations that something has justness may, of course, also be made without a reference to any criteria. In that case they are not „judgments" but „mere prizings", that is, arbitrary assessments. The subjective criteria of justness are a part of the valuating subject's *Weltanschauung*. They are developed through a person's life experience which have determined his attitudes towards his social environment and his ideas of how he would like the world to be. Those attitudes need not be conscious and explicit. But it should be possible somehow to discover them from the communicated contents of his typical cognitive, emotive, and conative acts. The variety of the world as well as of men's conceptions of the world determine the variety of the criteria of justness; hence there may be differences and conflicts between views as to what is the same person's due even though these views relate to essentially identical times, places, and circumstances.

The great number and variety of subjective criteria of justness by reference to which people make their judgments concerning justice renders it impossible to give a detailed account of them. An appropriate way of describing these criteria seems to be to relate the conceptions of what is a man's due to the principal types of *Weltanschauungen*. Such types are the individualistic, the collectivistic, and the transpersonal world outlooks as Gustav Radbruch[281] named them. A man with an individualistic outlook bases his judgment about justice and injustice on what he considers to serve best the purposes of an individual. The individual is for him the sole essential reality. Society for him is only a means to achieve the ends of the individual. A man with a collectivistic outlook bases his judgment about justice and injustice on what he considers to serve best the purposes of society. The individual apart from society is for him a member severed from a body, an entity of little value, actually a mere abstraction. Individuals, in order to exist, have to co-exist. The aims of individuals can only be properly achieved by promoting the aims of society. A man with a transpersonal outlook bases his judgment about justice and injustice on what he considers to serve best the purposes of entities created through the labours of the individual and society. These entities are culture, civilisation, spirit. From them both the individual and society derive their worth and in them they find their fulfilment of life. In the individualistic outlook, the emphasis lies on the due to be accorded to the individual. By according first the individual's due, society and transpersonal entities receive the share that justly ought to belong to them. In the collectivistic

---

[280] On the criteria of justness cf. J. Stone: The Province and Function of Law, 2nd. ed. 1950, 212, 375; id., Legal Controls of International Conflict, 1954, 54 ff.

[281] See G. Radbruch: Rechtsphilosophie, 4th ed. 1950, 146–155.

outlook, the emphasis lies on the due to be accorded to society. By according first the society's due, individuals and transpersonal entities receive what justly ought to belong to them. In the transpersonal outlook, the emphasis lies on the due to be accorded to transpersonal entities. Both the individual's and society's due are derivations from what is the *suum* of these transpersonal entities.

The above sketched *Weltanschauungen* stand to each other in multiple relations of tension and interpenetration. They are of such nature that none of them can be sustained as reasonable in its pure form. Hence, as described above, they are to be conceived not as empirical types but as ideal types[282]. In actuality these outlooks do not only occur in various shadings of their own[283] but also in combinations with each other in which their proper balance is sought. The criteria of justness to which they correspondingly give rise are determined by the components which make up the combinations and by the degree of harmony attained. The combined outlooks and the corresponding criteria of justness arise through the impact of various individualistic, collectivistic, and transpersonal ideas upon each other in the course of human communication[284], in which these take a more or less lasting objective form, that is, they become objectivised and thus become objective criteria of justness[285].

Of the objective criteria of justness the most important are principles provided by the norms of positive law. In these principles the elements of individualistic, collectivistic, and transpersonal outlook can be recognised, and the resultants of the process of their combination apprehended. The proposition that norms of positive law usually embody criteria of justness does not assert that all norms of positive law provide these criteria. There are legal norms of purely technical nature (for example, traffic regulations) which scarcely can be associated with justice at all, except as ancillary to other norms. Further there are

---

[282] On the problem of type concepts see A. Koort: Beiträge zur Logik des Typusbegriffes, in Acta et Commentationes Universitatis Tartuensis, B. Humaniora, 1936, vol. XXXVIII, 4; 1938, vol. XXXIX, 1.

[283] Thus collectivistic outlook can be universalistic, nationalistic, or one springing from group alignments smaller or larger than nation (provincialism, racialism, etc.).

[284] Cf. G. H. Mead: Mind, Self and Society, 1934, 319.

[285] Thought becomes objectivised in a complete act of communication. In such act the expression of a thought of the addresser is apprehended by the addressee as a sign of this thought and re-thought by him as the *significatum* of this *signum*. Only expressions in a permanent form constitute what is called „objective criteria of justness". Such criteria are objectivised, for example, in the expressions of positive law rules, written or unwritten. In the case of unwritten law, the expression of the criteria of justness consists in repeated patterns of manifested behaviour. Becoming objectivised, a thought becomes separated from its author, and starts an existence of its own, dependent on the social facts in the context of which it occurs. Positive law, too, as a set of norms providing criteria of justness is subject to all the vicissitudes of the objectivisation of thought. On the phenomenon of the objectivisation of thought see N. Hartmann: Das Problem des geistigen Seins, 2nd ed. 1949, 406—564.

norms of positive law to which hardly anyone is prepared to resort in performing the acts of the attribution of the just. Law occasionally gets out of touch with social reality and becomes petrified. While reforms are slow to come, it is a bane to everyone including the judges who have to apply it. The corresponding norms provide criteria of unjustness rather than criteria of justness. Finally there are tyrannical laws which do not exist for the sake of justice even to the tyrant himself, but derive such validity as they have from other considerations of lower axiotic dignity (for example, pleasure, convenience, or utility) than justice. Such laws do not „bind in conscience“[286].

There are some reasons, however, for doubting whether positive law is a set of norms providing criteria of justness at all. Such doubt arises from the fact that usually what is in accordance with this law is not called just but lawful or legal, which then is considered to coincide either with the just or with the unjust. But even though it is usually so, phrases which indicate that the norms of positive law are considered to provide criteria of justness, are not infrequent. Such phrases are „to do justice according to law“, „just remedy“, „without just cause and excuse“[287]. The fact that positive law provides criteria of justness does not prevent, however, positive law itself from being valuated by reference to criteria of justness provided by a different set of rules. So when a judge says that by giving a decision he has done justice according to law, he has employed positive law as norms providing criteria of justness. When his decision is criticised as being unjust, this can mean either that it is contended to be incorrect under the respective legal order or that in this criticism criteria of justness are employed which are provided by a set of norms different from those of the legal order in question[288] (given that the attribution of the just in this criticism is not altogether arbitrary).

The valuation of lawful decisions and even of the whole of a legal order as unjust, and contentions that certain other decisions and certain other legal order or orders would have justness, occur very often by reference to principles of natural law, which principles have played a prominent role as objective criteria of justness throughout the history

---

[286] Cf. St. Thomas Aquinus: Summa Theologica, I–II, 96–4.

[287] On these phrases see, for example, R. Pound: Justice according to Law, 1951, Part 3; R. F. V. Heuston (ed): Salmond on the Law of Torts, 11th ed. 1953, 31; and Bayley, J. in Bromage v. Prosser, 1925, 4 B. & C. 255.

[288] On the relation between justice and law cf. E. N. Garlan: Legal Realism and Justice, 1941, 21: „Not all law is just nor is justice law . . . Law may be either just or unjust; both judges and laws miss the mark, become petrified, and fail to meet needs. But law and justice cannot be intelligibly separated into radically different categories. They are distinctions within a common process, and neither can be entirely understood apart from the other. Law itself, apart from justice, is a blind mechanism and dangerously lunatic; justice apart from its potential embodiment in law, is idle fancy.“ See also ibid. 131: „ . . . the idea of justice is the entelechy of law . . .“ „ . . . justice is the teleological aspect of law.“

of Western civilisation. Natural law as a full set of definite or determinate norms is a presumed or postulated entity. It is not something unmistakably given. There may be an immutable order of Nature to which man and his society are subjected. It may be that *natura iuris ab hominis repetanda est natura*[289] or that law ought to correspond to the „nature of things"[290]. And the world may be a cryptogram of God's thoughts[291]. However, when man tries to understand this order, to apprehend this nature, and to read this cryptogram, he has to employ his reasoning in order to interpret what is given to him. In this interpretation a great number and variety of conceptions of natural law emerge[292] and correspondingly a great number and variety of criteria of justness, each claiming absoluteness as embodying the right law. In these criteria, as in positive law, elements of individualistic, collectivistic, and transpersonal outlooks can be noticed. In the plurality and variety of the norms of natural law there are many which enjoy a rather universal acceptance. Many of such norms have found their way from natural law doctrines into positive law. The principles of human rights[293], humane penalties, of fair trial, etc. all have their origin in natural law thought. In the so-called principles of natural justice such as *nemo iudex in causa sua* and *audiatur et altera pars*[294] their natural law thought origin can be recognised even in their common English name „principles of natural justice". In the very generally accepted principles of natural law, certain deeply felt needs of men and their societies are reflected[295],

[289] See G. Del Vecchio: Lehrbuch der Rechtsphilosophie, 2nd ed. edited and transl. by F. Darmstaedter, 1951, 589, quoting Cicero. For a contemporary conception of the nature of man see P. W. Kurtz: Human Nature, Homeostasis, and Value, 1956, 17, Philosophy and Phenomenological Research, 36, at 42 ff. and passim.

[290] On the nature of things as a legal-metaphysical problem see G. Radbruch: Die Natur der Sache als juristische Denkform, in Festschrift zu Ehren Rudolf Launs, 1948, 157 ff., esp. 162. See also E. Fechner: Rechtsphilosophie, 1956, 146–151.

[291] See K. Jaspers: Von der Wahrheit, 1947, in which work this is a recurrent thought. See also L. Lavelle: Traité des Valeurs, 1953, vol. I, 661.

[292] On this variety see H. Ryffel: Naturrecht, 1944, 37–129; J. Messner: Das Naturrecht, 1950, 83–95. Cf. A. Brecht: Relative and Absolute Justice, in M. D. Forkosch (ed.): The Political Philosophy of Arnold Brecht, 1950, 21–48, at 26. On the ambiguity of the notion „natural law" see E. Wolf: Das Problem der Naturrechtslehre, 1955, passim.

[293] On the problem of human rigths see UNESCO's symposium: Human Rights, 1949; G. Jellinek: Die Erklärung des Menschen- und Bürgerrechtes, 4th ed. 1927; J. Maritain: Les Droits de l'Homme et la Loi Naturelle, 1945; H. Lauterpacht: International Law and Human Rights, 1950.

[294] On the relation of these principles of judicial impartiality and fairness to justice see Garlan, op. cit. 76–88.

[295] Cf. L. L. Fuller: American Legal Philosophy at Mid-Century, 1954, 6 Journal of Legal Education, 457, at 481, who says that „If there are constancies and regularities that persist through a change in social forms these must reflect some constancy in the nature of man himself". On Fuller's conception of the nature of man see ibid. 472 ff.

needs clarified and expressed in the process of human communication[296] in the relative matters. In this process the sense of axiotic evidence of the valuating subjects becomes awakened with respect to the rightness of the attributions of the just and the unjust[297].

Neither the criteria of justness objectivised in positive law nor the objectivisations of these criteria in natural law doctrines can have the claim that they are absolute, perfectly reasonable, ultimate criteria of justness[298]. Indeed, on the contrary, what is absolute may still be directly irrelevant or even repugnant to human purposes[299]. Not everything that is objectivised is definitely reasonable. What is ultimate axiotically appears to be unachievable, at any rate, to *homo phenomenon*. However, the striving for definitely reasonable, ultimate criteria of justness is not without a purpose. The circumstance that such criteria are not something to be proved but only to be sincerely believed in, something to be assumed and contended about[300], suggests that man's struggle for their recognition ought to be carried out with an attitude which may be named circumspect solicitude, or more shortly — care, the notion of which attitude can perhaps be apprehended in the notion of *δικαιοσύνη*, the essence of Dike. The struggle for the attainment of objective criteria of justness and for their general recognition needs to be like a struggle for love. Dike will flee as love will withdraw when the object of one's desire is pursued with excessive clamour and in an unchivalrous spirit.

Since the ultimate criteria of justness are hidden from man and since satisfactory objective criteria of justness are not always available, Lord Denning's view that right-minded men are those on whose judgment men should rely in seeking justice[301] calls for attention. In

---

[296] Cf. H. Kelsen: What Is Justice? 1957, 7.

[297] The sense of axiotic evidence becomes dimmed in the contrary process of the breakdown of human communication. It need not, however, be affected by the violation and defiance of the principles in question. In them it rather may become accentuated.

[298] For a list of writers who have offered absolute standards of justice in our century and for concise presentation of their respective views see A. Brecht: Representative Advocates of Absolute Principles, in Forkosch (ed.), op. cit. 83–94.

[299] Cf. the words of Paul Valéry about „the real in its pure state" expressed in his book Eupalinos, 1924, 53: *„Le réel, à l'état pur, arrêt instantément le coeur . . . Une goutte suffit, de cette lymphe glaciale, pour détendre dans un âme, les ressorts et la palpitation du désir, exterminer toute espérances, ruiner tous les dieux qui étaient dans notre sang."*

[300] The road of human endeavour leading towards final understanding and towards realisation of worthwhile values appears to be always devious. *Homo viator* can strive for certainty only through doubt, for a fuller apprehension and realisation of values only through less complete apprehension of them. He must meet limit-situations to surmise the depths of his existence, must experience failures of his empirical Self to move towards the horizon of his authentic Self and must perhaps know forsakenness to find God.

[301] See A. Denning: The Road to Justice, 1955, 4.

every considerable human community there are men who excel in insight, knowledge, and moral qualities. Such men may be generally accepted as those who — by applying their subjective criteria of justness — would be competent to judge what is justice in the cases where the recourse to objective criteria of justness would be of no avail[302]. Such men are the arbiters of justice. Besides acting to fill gaps where objective criteria of justness are absent or defective, the arbiters of justice offer a possibility for the achievement of social peace by their judgments where it is threatened by issues of justice otherwise left at large. It may be easier to agree who should act as an arbiter of justice than on what is justice in a given case at issue. The authority of the arbiter may cause his decisions on disputes about justice to be accepted even by those who otherwise would regard decisions of the same content as unjust[303].

Whom to accept as an arbiter of justice presents, however, a problem of considerable difficulty. This acceptance implies a valuation which, like all valuations, can be objective, subjective, or purely arbitrary. To exclude arbitrariness here, the existence of „right-mindedness", which according to Lord Denning is the essential quality of the arbiters of justice, must be ascertained by reference to certain criteria. Finding the norms which would provide satisfactory criteria of right-mindedness appears to be an impossible task if right-mindedness is to mean a total excellence of mind. Persons who excel in knowledge, in common sense, in saintliness, or in other particular high intellectual or moral qualities may not be difficult to find. But those who combine the qualities which

---

[302] It may be noted that judges are generally reluctant to assume the responsibility of applying their subjective criteria of justness. As Helen Silving has rightly observed „a judge will more readily include in his decisions not supported by positive authority . . . the ‚law of reason' or ‚law of nature' . . . It is easier for him to say ‚natural justice demands' than to say ‚I believe it to be right'". See her article: The Twillight Zone of Positive and Natural Law, 1955, 43, California Law Review, 477, at 497 ff.

[303] A further significance of the arbiters of justice as men who occupy high judicial positions in a State lies in their role of the so-called social engineering. Insofar as they actually are men of high mental qualities, they may be trusted to take due notice of social interests pressing for recognition, to weigh them properly, and to give them legal effect in disputes about justice. These men — to use the words of Arthur E. Sutherland — „save us as individuals from our collective hasty intemperance or, more frequently, from our own simple lack of foresight. Amid the clamour and contention of the crowd it is a comfortable thing that we still have the wisdom to set apart for ourselves these calm judicial guardians, whose duty it is always to seek the just rule for our common lives". See his work The Law and One Man among Many, 1956, 97. We are still far from being able to perform the tasks of social engineering by completely rational methods. But intuitive faculties of trained and sincere minds may give satisfactory *ad hoc* solutions for the problem how to shape our social life. On the concept of social engineering see R. Pound: Interpretation of Legal History, 1923, 152—165; id.: An Introduction to the Philosophy of Law, 2nd ed. 1954, 47; Stone: Province, 771 ff., 782; R. Field and S. P. Simpson: Social Engineering through Law . . . , 1947, 22, New York University Law Review, 145—193.

would make a man totally right-minded are likely not to exist at all. Being outstanding in one particular respect does not exclude a man from being mediocre or even poor in another respect. Human experience tends to show that nobody is or can be a total genius[304], not at least in the present historical situation when mastering a special field of knowledge or possessing adequate skill in a special field of activity requires extreme specialisation of effort. Full wisdom is rare in our time as it has always been, but even merely comprehensive wisdom is what someone perhaps could possess only in past, less complicated times. It would be wise not to expect such wisdom from anyone as long as the human mind and its problems remain essentially the same as they are now.

Assuming that only partial wisdom may be expected from the arbiters of justice, the problem arises as to what are the principles for determining who would be the right man to decide the issues of justice in a particular case or in particular cases. It seems that a rather elaborate set of criteria is required in order to secure workable principles for selecting the arbiters of justice. One of the most important existing sets of the objective criteria for this selection is the set of principles determining the appointment of judges of the superior courts and the allocation of judicial work to them[305]. In all stable civilised contemporary communities the judges of superior courts are formally required to be men of thorough legal training and of high moral standards. But neither of these qualities warrants completely that they will be the right men to act as arbiters of justice. In the doing of that justice for which law does not provide criteria, the principles of existing law and conventional morality, to which the judges must feel attached, may prove considerable obstacles in certain dynamic states of social reality. Apart from these principles, the other important set of objective criteria for selecting the arbiters of justice is the principles by which the legislative organs of States are created. These principles seem to give even less assurance to the existence of the right-mindedness (to which Lord Denning refers) in the persons who act as legislators than the principles according to which judges are selected warrant the right-mindedness of judges. If to a considerable extent, nevertheless, right-minded men appear to occupy the positions of the arbiters of justice in civilised communities, this appears to be largely due to circumstances other than the enacted criteria of their selection.

Both the objective criteria of justness and the objective criteria of right-mindedness by which the arbiters of justice are selected have been subject to considerable criticism by political scientists and philosophers. These have propounded criteria competing with those that already exist, often claiming that their views are based on natural law and right reason. The force of conviction behind these views has depended on

---

[304] A person who is a genius in certain respect may be completely incapable and unreliable in other respects. It is not even precluded that a person who may be regarded as a genius is affected by insanity.

[305] On these principles see Denning, op. cit. 10—32.

their intrinsic merits as well as on the conditions of social life in the particular time and place, and possessing this force, they have often become incorporated in positive law and morality. Some of these criteria suggested by the political writers may be considered the best for the particular time and place, but there appears to be no sufficient reason to regard them as possessing a transcendent dignity. If the ultimate criteria of justness and right-mindedness ever come within the ambit of human vision at all, there appears to be no test which would exclude doubt about their disputed claims to this dignity.

15. Remarks on the Psychology of Justice

The psychological problems of justice are, strictly, not problems of the fundamental principles of justice. But as they belong to important empirical circumstances in which these principles are grounded, some remarks about them may be made in the present essay. The study of the psychology of justice[306] may be expected to reveal, why there are a great number and variety of ideas of justice, and why the realisation of justice is a painful process.

The experience of the just and of the criteria of justness is a specific experience only in a mind which has attained sufficient intellectual maturity. In an immature mind there is an amorphous mass of pleasure-pain sensations and a welter of desires and aversions which are organised only into very confused notions of values. Such a mind commingles various positive values with each other and various negative values with each other, employing their notions interchangeably. This mind is particularly liable to make arbitrary valuations; is capable perhaps only of arguing but not of reasoning about values. A sufficient intellectual maturity for the experiences of the just and of criteria of justness is attained when man is consciously seeking what is his due in relation to his fellow men, when he is wondering what this due is, when he is demanding it consistently and struggling purposefully for its recognition, whatever his particular version of the due to be accorded may be.

In the study of the psychodynamics of justice[307] the following facts may be observed: A new-born child has only instinctive responses to inner and outer stimuli. He does not appear to differentiate himself from the surrounding world[308]. When the development of the child has reached the stage of an ego-consciousness, he is able to contrast himself with the rest of the world, and to face his environment, apprehending

---

[306] On the psychology of justice cf. the section entitled *„Die Psychologie des Rechtsmenschen"* by G. Radbruch in his treatise Rechtsphilosophie, 4th ed. 1950, 196—204.

[307] On the psychodynamics of the ideas of justice see J. Piaget: Le Jugement Moral chez l'Enfant, 1932, 225—373; F. R. Bienenfeld: Rediscovery of Justice, 1947, esp. pp. 18—55. See also W. D. Lamont: The Principles of Moral Judgment, 1946, 137 ff.

[308] He is intimately a part of it like a raindrop on a leaf, a tree in the garden, or a bird in the air.

it as being friendly, hostile, or indifferent to him. In the early years of his ego-conscious life, the child considers himself the most central person of all. Although he considers his parents central too, even attributing omnipotence to them, they are still subordinate to him. Implicit in the child's attitudes there appears to be the idea that parents exist only to procure his enjoyment. The dominant affective attitude of a child in the first years of his life is self-love. He admires himself narcissistically, and claims his mother's and father's exclusive love. When he finds that his parents' love belongs also to his brothers and sisters and to each other[309], he feels resentment, the extreme form of which are death wishes[310] towards everyone who frustrates the attainment of the objective of his affections. Insofar as this child can conceive of something being due to him or to other persons, he considers that everything he desires is due to him; to other persons is due only what serves the attainment of his aims. The „*Weltanschauung*" of the child in this stage of development is individualistic to the extreme.

This picture of a child in the narcissistic period — and this is a period which every normally developing child goes through — may appear to be shocking[311], but there is also a charm in it if the child's attitudes are considered against the background of his innocence and in the light of what may develope from these humble moral beginnings. Men who achieve the highest peaks of heroism and saintliness were once such children. There is nothing deplorable in the fact that children in their early years are what they are, but it is alarming that there are cases of arrested development or of moral regression where the narcissistic phase may extend into adulthood, and may even never be overcome. In these persons perverted or crude conceptions of justice may be noticed. In the normal development of the child, the narcissistic period sooner or later passes. The child learns to recognise the rights of other egos, first perhaps as a necessary evil, later, however, as a matter of course, as something not to be regretted or resented. The parents' attitudes to the world as well as the attitudes of those other grown-ups with whom the child comes into contact, become introjected[312] in his mind as dictates of his conscience[313]. Judging what is his due and the due of other persons now

---

[309] On justice and the relations between children and parents see Bienenfeld, op. cit. 27–40. On justice and the relations between children and their brothers and sisters see ibid. 18–27.

[310] The most important role in the children's death wishes is played, according to Wilhelm Stekel, by poison. See his treatise Compulsion and Doubt (transl. by E. Gutheil, 1950), vol. II, p. 551.

[311] Cf. G. Allport: Becoming, 1955, 28: „ . . . at the age of two the child is, when measured by standards applied to adults, an unsocialised horror."

[312] On the arisal of Superego through the mechanism of introjection see, for example, O. Fenichel: The Psychoanalytical Theory of Neurosis, 1945, 109, 470.

[313] On the growth of conscience see Allport, op. cit. 68–74. On the infantile conscience see E. H. Erikson: Kindheit und Gesellschaft, 1957, 236. Erikson says that the fact that human conscience remains partially infantile

takes place in accordance with these dictates. Thus the child learns to have compassion and care, but sometimes also indifference and cruelty towards others, or he may acquire the habit of being confused and inconsistent in his moral behaviour — depending on the nature of the influences of his social environment. Arrested development and regression may take place also in relation to this stage when conscience develops as a result of parental and other social authority[314]. There are people even at an advanced age who seem not to have attained a proper moral maturity, still living in the enclosure of ideas that belong to someone else. Their criteria of justness frequently are those which come from an identifiable person accepted as an authority. Such people accept these criteria as principles for their attributions of the just and unjust *because* they come from this authority.

In late adolescence and in early adulthood the young man normally experiences a need for emancipation from his parents and their substitutes. He wants to leave home and to start an independent life, and objects to the pressure of moral guidance offered by parents and teachers. Often he considers their moral principles outdated. In this stage of development the experience of the just is usually intense and distinct, but the criteria of justness, which developed from the child's individualistic „outlook" towards a collectivistic „outlook" of the early adolescence, become confused. The constructive principles according to which he and the world should live have not yet become crystallised in his young mind. So his attitude tends to be a protest, a saying of no to the old for the sake of something new and better to be created, of which he, however, has no clear idea. But even in his attitude of protest and in his lack of clarity about what he is actually striving for, he is moving towards a collectivistic outlook with respect to his criteria of justness. There are cases of arrested development and regression also in relation to this stage. Persons of mature age who excel in destructive criticism of social situations, but are unable to advance any constructive ideas about them that would constitute any worthwhile aims, are by no means rare.

Having achieved mature adulthood, man has not only himself and his family for objects of his care but, to a certain extent, also his town, his country, and even the world. He recognises the idea of justice as an important regulative principle of social life, without whose realisation to a reasonable degree his role as a husband and father, as a citizen, and as a member of human race is unpleasant and dangerous, if not impossible. Thus his thoughts become concerned with justice; he adopts certain current views on it as his own, and may even join groups fighting for the version of the idea of justice which appeals to him. His idea of justice may not be for him only a norm for regulating his behaviour with respect

---

throughout the entire life of man is the core of the human tragedy. For the psycho-analytical conception of the development of conscience see Fenichel, op. cit. 102–113.

314 On conscience in relation to ethics see E. Fromm: Man for Himself, 1947, 141–172.

to the objects of his care but may become an object of care itself, an object to be defended, to be realised, and even to be died for. In this stage of development or in the lower stages, the majority of people remain. Seeking to transcend this stage by making the *idea* of justice which one has and in which one believes, an object of one's care in order to refine it, to elevate it, and to allot to it its proper place among other norms, is the concern only of very few minds.

The great number and variety of the criteria of justness and of the ideas of justice can now be stated as being occasioned by the impact of various environmental circumstances on the human mind. This impact will, of course, produce different effects according to the constitutional differences of persons such as sensitiveness, greater or lesser inner stability, and intelligence (insofar as they are not acquired). The ideas of justice are largely carried on from generation to generation as a precious inheritance or as a serious disease; in both cases they have a great power of resistance to efforts to remove them. In the mature stage of adulthood, justice is mainly an object of contention and strife, but not of circumspect solicitude, not an object of Care. The psychological facts relating to justice suggest that the unity of experiences of the just, the criteria of justness, and the ideas of justice which may be achieved in ideologically divided humanity is greatly dependent on the common life experiences of every member of it. These life experiences can be made less divergent than they are now through continued and increased efforts to remove the barriers of human communication, but it is unreasonable to expect that any considerable unity can be achieved, even if such a unity is desirable.

An account of the psychology of justice must also take notice of the basic emotion „anxiety" in relation to the experiences of the just, criteria of justness, and the ideas of justice[315]. When a child is punished or reprimanded, it is thereby frequently imposed on his mind that he should have done something that was somebody's due and avoided what was contrary to it. Doing injustice thus becomes associated in his mind with a fear of punishment. When direct parental authority is replaced with conscience, doing injustice is associated with anxiety which need not have a conscious object, because the punisher and the nature of punishment has vanished from the consciousness along with the disappearance of the conscious parents' imago and their authority, to make room for the Superego[316]. This anxiety often constructs for itself an object in the form of entities such as God and Fate, who allot sufferings in this world or in the hereafter as a just retribution for failure to be just. The nameless anxiety from which some people on some occasions suffer is connected

[315] On the significance of the phenomenon of anxiety („fear") for man's social behaviour and for his attitudes to justice see H. Kelsen: What Is Justice? 1957, 22 ff.

[316] On the Superego („conscience") in relation to man's social behaviour see R. West: Conscience and Society, 1945, passim. See also A. Campbell Garnett: The Moral Nature of Man, 1952, 161–165, esp. at 163.

with a vague notion that something which ought to have been done[317] has not been done, that someone's due has not been accorded. To escape from this anxiety all Freudian mechanisms[318], such as repression, displacement, and rationalisation, are resorted to, mechanisms which are particularly operative in neurotic disturbances. Escape from one's responsibility into neuroses is an important mode of absenting oneself or moving further away from one's authentic Self; it is a mode of inauthenticity. However, escape from anxiety occasioned by the unjustness of which men sense themselves to be guilty need not always be the escape into what is called neurosis. It may also be the resort to typical attitudes and conduct of „everydayness[319]", which are not necessarily of psychopathological character. To these belongs „mere talk", a behaviour by which a person's anxiety and inner tension are converted into a motoric activity of speech organs purporting to convey thoughts but achieving this purpose to a poor degree. Another mode of „everydayness" is recourse to the authority and protection of the anonymous entity of people's opinion, which opinion is actually an opinion of no one, even though the recourse to it is made in the form: „This is so because *one* says that it is so." Finally, the „everydayness" of the unjust man eventuates also in the mode of a restless seeking in something new solutions for the problems arising from one's unjust behaviour. In this restless seeking man neglects the assimilation of gathered experiences and their continuity. In all modes of inauthenticity manifesting themselves in the behaviour of the unjust man, his estrangement from *Dike* takes place, and he associates himself with her adversaries: *Eris, Hybris, Dysnomia, Lethe,* and *Amphilogiai* — all arisen, fatherless, from the essence of *Nyx,* the chthonic deity of darkness, of gloom.

16. About the Metaphysics of Justice: Some Reflections

To enter upon the metaphysics of justice may seem unnecessary. Metaphysics, as it has been conceived, is a quest for the ultimate causes and ultimate ends; it is speculation upon the transintelligible, upon the supreme value, upon Being as such[320]. There are many who feel no inclination whatsoever towards such an enterprise, and able arguments

---

[317] Cf. the conception of justice in Plotinus, according to whom justice means doing one's work and fulfilling one's task. See R. Harder (ed.): Plotins Schriften, 1930, vol. I, p. 187, and the Platonic conception of justice as doing one's task (see supra s. 4).

[318] For a concise statement of the Freudian mechanisms see S. H. Kraines: The Therapy of the Neuroses and Psychoses, 2nd ed. 1943, 56—84.

[319] On „everydayness" as a mode of inauthenticity see M. Heidegger: Sein und Zeit, 7th ed. 1953, 126—130; 167—180. His terms for the specific modes treated in the text are *„das Gerede"* („mere talk"), *„das Man"* („the one"), and *„die Neugier"* (or rather *„die Neu-gier"*, meaning the craving and seeking for novelty).

[320] And upon Nothingness. See for the basic question of metaphysics as conceived by Martin Heidegger: *„Warum ist überhaupt Seiendes und nicht vielmehr Nichts?"* in his work Einführung in die Metaphysik, 1953, 1—39, in which pages the question occurs as a recurrent theme.

have been advanced that it is impossible or foolish[321]. But it can be retorted that metaphysical ponderings are not altogether idle[322]. That there is no *designatum* for metaphysical *significata* can hardly be seriously contended, and if it were so contended, this could be done only by notions and statements which would themselves prove metaphysical. Man's metaphysical quest seems to have at least this purpose, that through it he articulates his attitudes towards what is unknown and unknowable to him; and through his constant failure to achieve any assured results in this metaphysical speculation he may come to a better awareness of his own limits and to a better appreciation of other people's attitudes towards the ultimate.

When notions of justice are condemned as metaphysical, the reproach is often made that they are empty[323]. This reproach, even if founded, scarcely holds for all metaphysical notions. Some of these, for example, „the Absolute“ and „God“, seem to be characterised by extreme fullness. Whether empty or full, metaphysical notions and statements are nevertheless not irrelevant for human pursuits. Their emptiness and their fullness, being beyond man's comprehension, provide him with references which are detached from the world in whose complex and confused situations he is entangled. Metaphysical words are like words of prayer, and as such they are able to invoke a condition of unworldliness in man which is necessary, on many occasions, for the finding of his place and his way as a dweller and wayfarer in this world[324]. Admittedly, metaphysics has much in common with religion, but to condemn it for this reason is hardly reasonable. The religious attitude appears to be something which neither science nor philosophy, neither art nor technology can render superfluous — unless indeed these become themselves a cult akin to religion.

Detachment achieved through metaphysical notions and speculations lifts man out of the standing in which his everydayness places him and leads him to points of understanding from which he may be able to regard the world with greater clarity and in better perspective[325]. Metaphysics is thus relevant for man's transcending his phenomenal Self

[321] As typical contemporary works expressing anti-metaphysical attitudes see H. Reichenbach: The Rise of Scientific Philosophy, 1951, esp. 3—114; A. J. Ayer: Language, Truth and Logic, 1948; J. Wisdom: Other Minds, 1952, esp. the essay Metaphysics, pp. 236—259.

[322] Cf. S. E. Toulmin: The Place of Reason in Ethics, 1950, 209.

[323] See, for example, V. Lundstedt: Law and Justice, in P. Sayre (ed.): Interpretations of Modern Legal Philosophies, 1947, 450—483, esp. p. 450.

[324] In a world which he has not chosen but in which he finds himself and to which he has to adapt himself by modifying things-in-the-world and himself as a man-in-the-world. Cf. in this context Heidegger's notion of „thrownness“ *(Geworfenheit)* in his treatise Sein und Zeit, 7th ed. 1953, 175—180.

[325] Cf. O. Brusiin: Über das juristische Denken, 1951, 4: *„Der Mensch ist ein Wesen, das ein fundamentales Bedürfnis hat, sich auf überempirisches, objektiv nicht Verifizierbares zu beziehen.“* Cf. also ibid. 12, 154, 162. And cf. E. Fechner: Rechtsphilosophie, 1956, 278 ff.; Ph. Lersch: Aufbau der Person, 1951, 131—157.

and for approach to the *ek-stasis* of his noumenal authentic Self[326]. Hence the metaphysical quest for justice need not be an aberration. The „Categorical Imperative", the „Golden Rule", the precept „to everyone his due" and other formulae of justice alleged to be empty[327], perform an important function even in their emptiness. They carry with them an emotional quality, a pathos, perhaps no less intense than the pathos which the objective, the real[328], the concrete, and the full are capable of carrying, and thus create the disposition of the mind, *animi affectio,* in which the just as a subjective value is experienced. In this *animi affectio* appear to lie higher potentialities for mastering social problems than lie in the forgetfulness of justice arising from ignorance, from not-caring, and from anti-metaphysical attitudes. It is from this disposition of justice that springs its power — adapting the dictum of Parmenides — to hold within bounds the creation and destruction in society.

It is incontestable that metaphysics as a science is inconceivable, insofar as sciences are regarded as being concerned with phenomena the propositions about which can be verified. Metaphysical statements are unverifiable by their very nature: no verification is conceivable of what is beyond our knowledge, is inscrutable, ineffable. Metaphysical statements do not thus constitute theses which can be defended or refuted by cogent arguments. They are hypo-theses[329] which can only satisfy

---

[326] The phrase „*ek-stasis* of his noumenal Self" is intended to convey that this Self is an entity of assymptotic, or rather periechontological character. The noumenal Self is the surmised entity to which the empirical Self, that is, our consciousness as it exists in our actual experience, can only infinitely approach but which it can never reach. In certain mental conditions, man may have the impression that his mind has effected a „break-through" and apprehended his noumenal Self or has become „one" with it. This condition has been denoted by the notion „ecstasy". The metaphysical notion of *ek-stasis* has, however, no essential connection with the notion of ecstasy. It is based on the original intuition of „*ek-*", which signifies „outside", and „*stasis*", which signifies „standing". With this original intuition of the word the idea of the assymptotic or periechontological character of the standing-outside is connected in the notion „*ek-stasis*". With the notion „*ek-stasis*" as understood here cf. Karl Jaspers' notion „*Existenz*" in his treatise Von der Wahrheit, 1947, 76. On the conception of periechontology see ibid. 160.

[327] On the emptiness of these rules see H. Kelsen: What Is Justice? 1957, 13–18. On the Golden Rule see P. Tillich: The New Being, 1955, 30–33. According to Tillich, „Love makes justice just" (p. 32) and „makes Golden Rule possible" (p. 33).

[328] This pathos is particularly manifest in the works of the Scandinavian legal realists. See, for example, A. Hägerström: Inquiries into the Nature of Law and Morals (ed. by K. Olivecrona, transl. by C. D. Board, 1953); A. Ross: Towards a Realistic Jurisprudence, 1946; V. Lundstedt, article cited supra n. 323.

[329] The hyphenation in „hypo-thesis" is employed to indicate that the word occurs here as signifying a proposition *(thesis)* which is under or below *(hypo-)* the level of ordinary propositions. This being „under" or „below" is significant

the mind to a higher or lower degree. Even thus they give the mind a tentative and temporary hold in its efforts to reach beyond the empirical. The entities with which metaphysics is concerned are not those of the phenomenal world; they are noumena, the ultimate principles underlying phenomena. In dealing with noumenal entities by means of tentative statements which are hypo-theses, man wonders about the infinite background of everything, including himself[330]. From the points of understanding at which he may arrive through this wonder, no object with boundaries, perhaps no object at all, comes into his view; the entities apprehended in metaphysical speculation are periechontological: they have no boundaries. The points of understanding attained in the metaphysical quest open only *vistas* towards the *horizons* of man's *intimité spirituelle*[331] and of the reality which sustains and surrounds him[332], so that his anxiety and love, hope and faith, knowledge and ignorance may be experienced in serenity and may appear as something always to be transcended in the infinite matrix of the totality of Being. Metaphysical experiences, lacking objectivity, are also devoid of a definite purpose and meaning. But in the diffuse light of these experiences man becomes aware, against the penumbral background[333] of the finite entities apprehended, of the limited value of what appears to him objective and of the transitory character of his „definite" purposes and meanings. Thus metaphysical questionings and metaphysical experiences are conducive to the spirit of openmindedness and tolerance liberating the energies of men's minds and allowing them to accomplish more than they can accomplish when these minds are constantly earthbound in the fetters of the perceptible, objective, and definite[334].

The mind contemplating what appears to it from its metaphysical points of understanding does not cognise but surmises. Surmising in the metaphysical sense means an extrapolation into transcendence; it means

---

in two respects: (1) In contrast to ordinary propositions, metaphysical propositions are unverifiable on principle. Hypotheses as employed, for example, in science are always verifiable at least on principle, and the efforts of scientists are directed to their conversion into proven propositions. (2) Metaphysical propositions as hypo-theses refer to circumstances which are, in a certain sense, underlying the phenomenal world. The word „hypo-thesis" is thus linked with the word „understanding", which in the present essay has been employed to refer to an awareness which is not a full cognitive awareness but which nevertheless is a basic cognitive state of the mind.

330 Cf. Edmund Husserl's characterisation of phenomenological philosophy as „man's whole occupation with himself in the service of universal reason" See E. Hu(sserl), *sub voce* „Phenomenology" in Encyclopaedia Britannia, 1953, vol. XVII, p. 702.

331 To use a phrase of Louis Lavelle. See his work De l'Intimité Spirituelle, 1955, 31, and note the title of this work.

332 Cf. A. N. Whitehead: Essays in Science and Philosophy, 1947, 77 ff., 106.

333 Cf. ibid. 122.

334 Cf. L. L. Fuller: The Law in Quest of Itself, 1940, 109.

a „pointing beyond[335]“, a moving from a given basis of experiencing in the manner determined by this basis towards the open horizons of the unknown into a domain where there are no cognitive roads. Since the metaphysical surmising means the mind's moving in an *aporia,* the experience of surmising cannot be described but only intimated[336]. This intimating cannot always rely on the ways of scholarly expression, but has often to resort to metaphorical indication, that is, to poetical expression. Hence metaphysics, more than other branches of philosophy, has borne a resemblance to poetry. The intimating metaphysical expressions do not communicate knowledge of the entities surmised but rather of the conditions in which surmising can take place in the privacy of the mind engaged in metaphysical speculations. Because the metaphysical intimating ultimately refers to the *intimité spirituelle* of man, which appears to defy any objectivisation, metaphysics bears a resemblance to mysticism.

The metaphysical problems of justice emerge when justice is apprehended in relation to God, to the Absolute, and to natural law. Being absolutely just has been regarded as one of the transcendent attributes of God[337]. From Him, the Supreme Lawgiver, the eternal principles of natural law have been conceived to irradiate, these principles constituting the absolute criteria of justness. Since God, the Absolute, the Eternal, and the Transcendent are noumena: entities the contemplation of which involves a frustration agreeing with few minds, man's concern with these entities has resulted in attaching to them ideas of little or no metaphysical content. Thus God has been conceived sometimes as wonderful and sometimes as terrible, as a ruler and as a companion, as a loving father who takes care of all human affairs and as an impassive artisan who having done the work of creation has forsaken man and „condemned him to freedom[338]“. From this humanised, phenomenal God man has asked the possible and the impossible; has flattered Him, cajoled Him, but also cursed Him and abandoned Him. The phenomenal *denotata* of the notions of God, by which He is not apprehended as a noumenal entity, have been one reason for the frustration in achieving agreement on the ideas of justice and on the criteria of justness.

But the quest for absolute justice cannot be rendered pointless by the frustrations which this quest brings to man. The Absolute, being the noumenal *situs* for everything, is also the metaphysical background for justice. Our bonds with this *situs,* this background are inseverable. To relegate the Absolute to Non-being is of no avail, because Non-being appears necessarily to be. To show that all arguments about the Absolute

---

[335] On „pointing beyond“, surmising, and understanding cf. L. Wittgenstein: Philosophical Investigations (transl. by G. E. M. Anscomb, 1953), 83 ff., §§-208–210, p. 89 §-245, p. 143 §-527.

[336] On „intimating“ cf. Wittgenstein, op. cit. 87 §-237.

[337] On the idea that justness is an essential quality of gods in Greek religion see H. Kelsen: Society and Nature, 1943, 187 ff.

[338] A phrase of Jean-Paul Sartre. See his treatise L'Etre et le Néant, 41st ed. 1953, 515.

are unverifiable does not abolish it. If the expression „the Absolute" is said to be meaningless, meaninglessness[339] calls for metaphysical attention; if the Absolute is said to be nothing, nothingness emerges as an enormous metaphysical problem[340]. Persistent denial of the Absolute leads to a whirl of endless regression, the totality of which still refers to the Absolute; it leads to an endless welter of relations, absolute too in their totality[341]. But man being *of* the Absolute, *in* the Absolute, and perhaps *for* the Absolute, can dispose it as little as he can dispose *of* it. Since the Absolute is unfathomable, in seeking answers to questions concerning absolute justice man is only absolutising his own relative solutions, arrogating to them an unwarranted dignity. And even if absolute justice should become, in an *unio mystica,* an experience to someone, the Absolute retains its sublime silence towards other people who have not shared this experience and may be incapable of ever attaining it. So a man communing with the Absolute must expect difficulties in communicating what this communing has meant; he has a poor chance to be understood by others, even to be listened to[342].

Illumination about absolute justice and bringing its idea to the cave of the unillumined world thus may mean nothing else than throwing one more idea of justice into the world, even provided that this illumination were something more than an illusion. In the world of „everydayness", the ideas of justice, whatever their origin and ultimate worth become forces engendering strife. Even the highest ideas of justice — like man's ideals of felicity, eternity and God — have been fought for and fought against with all the methods of depravity and horror tha man is capable of devising. In his struggle for the sake of a justice which he considers ultimate, divine, absolute, man is in constant dange of falling into *hybris*. The *hybris* of justice is injustice, apart fron being also an anti-value for other values of high axiotic dignity. Tc be constantly in situations of struggle is something from which mar cannot escape[343]. The nature of the struggle in which he is engaged is however, not subjected to the rule of *Moira;* man appears to have som competence to determine the means by which he fights and the manne in which he conducts the fight. The struggle for the realisation of a idea of justice, too, can be subjected to *temperamenta,* that is, t restraints.

Living in a world where there is a plurality of conflicting ideas c justice, among which none may represent absolute or perfect justice

---

339 On the problem of meaninglessness see M. White: Toward Reunio in Philosophy, 1956, 101, 104.

340 This is the principal theme in M. Heidegger: Was ist Metaphysik 1929.

341 On the problem of the Absolute see F. H. Bradley: Appearance an Reality, 9th impr. 1930, 403—452.

342 Cf. A. Campbell Garnett: The Moral Nature of Man, 1952, 41.

343 Struggle is, according to Karl Jaspers, one of the so-called limi situations. See his treatise Philosophie, 2nd ed. 1948, 494—505. See al. L. Lavelle: Le Moi et Son Destin, 1936, 111.

man's task is to find a procedure in which one idea of justice could be converted into an axiotic circumstance whereas the others would wait until their chance of realisation comes through the same procedure[344]. In the meantime the waiting ideas need not lie idle. They can play an active role as criteria by recourse to which actual situations of prevailing justice could be contended to be just or unjust. These criteria would then have the important role of helping to extinguish the life of the dominant idea of justice or of helping a change in this idea to come about.

The *eris* enflamed by the tension between the plurality of the ideas of justice suggests a need for an embracing balancing principle of human action which would govern the events and the outcome of the struggle in which man becomes engaged for the sake of particular ideas of justice. Since the sought principle is to be *regulative* of *human* action, it must be of less limited scope than justice as conceived by Anaximander and Parmenides, for whom it meant a balancing principle of cosmic events. On the other hand, this principle must be wider than justice as conceived by Aristotle and the philosophers after him, for whom justice meant a value relating to man's *social* behaviour. In the history of doctrine, a basis for the sought principle can perhaps be found in the Platonic notion of justice as the principle regulative of *all* human actions and attitudes[345]. An appropriate name for this principle is perhaps „Care" *(„Cura")*[346]. „Care" means a loving concern[347], a circumspect solicitude, a considerate affection; it means an emotion of both love and anxiety governed and transfigured under the norm of Reason. The pregnant word „Care" is employed to refer to man's care of himself, to his care with the means he applies, to his care about the ends he follows, and to his care for his fellow-creatures. The surmised afflatus of the emotion of Care may be intimated as the noësis, the noëmatic correlate of which is the supreme value, the *Summum Bonum*.

---

[344] Cf. Gustav Radbruch's view on the relation between democracy and relativism expressed in his treatise Rechtsphilosophie, 4th ed. 1950, 84. Cf. also Kelsen: What Is Justice? 23 ff. And cf. A. Boyce Gibson: Should Philosophers Be Kings? 1939, 30.

[345] In seeking a historical basis for the idea of *Cura* in the thoughts of ancient philosophers, I may quote Alfred North Whitehead's apt remark to be found in his work cited supra n. 332, p. 84: „The systematic thought of ancient writers is now nearly worthless; but their detached insights are priceless."

[346] For notions in contemporary philosophy that have a similarity with the notion of Care outlined in the text see, for example, *„Sorge"* in Heidegger: Sein und Zeit, 191—196; „the generalised, non-specific urge to creative and experimental living" in Campbell Garnett, op. cit. 148; „the All-Benevolent Will" in B. Perry: General Theory of Values, 1926, 682—687. Cf. also John Dewey's notion „caring-for" in his essay The Field of ‚Value', in R. Lepley (ed.): Value, 1949, 64—77, at 67 ff.

[347] On „concern" as an important quality of human life see C. I. Lewis: An Analysis of Knowledge and Valuation, 1946, 479.

The emotion of boundless Care, *Cura infinita,* to be experienced in this afflatus, may be intimated as the noësis which points to the subsistence of God[348], the Supreme Entity, the metabasis of the *Summum Bonum.* The philosophical notion of boundless Care, like all metaphysical notions, is necessarily vague, adumbrating something beyond exact definition and satisfactory clarification[349]. But being founded on the intuitive ground of man's actual experiences of care, it is a notion the content of which can be surmised by extrapolating from the known and shared experiences of care towards the limitless horizons encompassing any particular phase of these experiences.

The vague, indefinite, and horizonal character of the metaphysical notion of boundless Care[350], like the same character of the notion of ultimate justice[351], is not a sufficient reason to consider this notion irrelevant for human pursuits. The pathos which it carries constitutes an additional factor to the emotive force carried by the idea of absolute justice for holding within bounds the creation and destruction taking place in society. As a metaphysical notion, „*Cura infinita*" does not provide definite precepts for social behaviour. But the intimation of the open horizons of our cognition and conation which it imports may help us to understand better our human situation so that we could be delivered from harmful rigidity in our social attitudes and actions.

---

[348] Cf. Lavelle: Le Moi et Son Destin, 96: „*L'intimité même de l'Etre ne se livre à nous que dans le Souci.*"

[349] Cf. Whitehead, op. cit. 125.

[350] The notion „boundless Care" — like, for example, the notions „authentic Self", „Being", and „the Absolute" — is periechontological denoting entities which encompass the finite minds like horizons and are cognitively transcendent to them. As a periechontological notion, „boundless Care" is not capable of supporting steps of scientific reasoning. But even so it is not an irrelevant notion. It is capable of being an entity to which the inquirer's emotive and conative attention can be attached in his effort to advance knowledge and thereby other worthwhile aims. It carries the idea of a call for the attitudes which the enlightened man has learnt to treasure as essential for realising values of high axiotic dignity. Even though the notion „boundless Care" cannot be a bridge to anything, as the notions of empirical contents can be in syllogistic reasoning, it can serve us as an arrow carrying us towards what may lie as values in our cognitive, emotive, and conative horizons. On the impossibility to define the notion „boundless Care" cf. P. Tillich: Love, Power, and Justice, 1954, 3, who submits that the root meaning of love cannot be defined, but „must be described in its qualities and expressions".

[351] Ultimate justice as divine justice is beyond man's understanding; it is something „hidden in the mysterious wisdom of God". See Kelsen's exposition of St. Paul's conception of divine justice in his work What Is Justice? 12 ff. On the notion of divine justice see also G. Del Vecchio: Justice Divine et Humaine, 1955, 9, Revue Internationale de Defense Social, 1—10; E. Brunner: Gerechtigkeit, 1943, 54—64. And see Tillich: Love, Power, and Justice, 66: „God is not bound to the given proportion between merit and tribute. He can creatively change the proportion, and does it in order to fulfil those who according to proportional justice would be excluded from fulfilment. Therefore the divine justice can appear as plain injustice."

Denoting *caritas sapientis*[352], *amor amicitiae*[353], it may guide us in our search for situations in which the best achievable justice for the given social conditions would be realised. The noëmatic correlate of the noësis of *Cura infinita* which man's phenomenal Self may be capable of experiencing is the *Summum Bonum* indistinctly adumbrated, an aspect of God as *Deus Absconditus*. But even this experience appears to be a step on the road towards the *ek-stasis* of his authentic Self, the taking of which road surely is important in our axiotic strivings. God that remains hidden in our actual *cura* is not an irrelevant God to us[354]. Even this God we can approach with our reverence, worship and ultimate longing and leave to Him everything that is beyond our own powers to arrange. In response to this emotion of *cura* we may expect His grace[355], by which those things that *we* cannot achieve in the knowing and realising of justice will be given to us. This we may hope if we do not commit the act of sacrilege of trying to convert God's subsistence into an existence[356] in our everydayness. By this act we restrict the compass of our Care, and commit ourselves to damnation by adding one more demon to the conflicts in which we are engaged.

Sixth Discourse

Having come to the end of my inquiry into the fundamentals of justice, I now propose to look back and see where I have arrived. In so doing I find that I have covered a vast ground with long hasty strides, thus obtaining only percursory views of many relevant matters and passing over a number of problems of considerable significance. However, to sketch outlines of an intricate and extensive object of inquiry appears to be a permissible and not necessarily an idle approach to reality; I have taken no obligations to offer more than I have been able to give in my chapters and discourses. Of the problems which I could not help posing but did not manage to tackle, one especially looms large and commands my attention even at this final stage of the work[357]. This

---

[352] With the characterisation of *Cura* as *caritas sapientis* cf. W. Fuchs: Neoklassik in der Rechtsphilosophie, 1954, 92. Cf. also L. Lavelle: De l'Etre, 2nd ed. 1947, 34.

[353] On the notion of *amor amicitiae* see Duns Scotus: Opus Oxoniense, III, d. 27, qu. 1, n. 17; IV, d. 49, qu. 5, n. 3. See also id., II, d. 6, qu. 2, n. 3.

[354] Cf. Lavelle: Le Moi et Son Destin, 128: *„Il est secret parce qu'il veut que nous le cherchions. Mais s'il se cache, ce n'est pas pour nous dammer, c'est pour nous animer."*

[355] On the relations between justice and grace see G. Radbruch: Rechtsphilosophie, 4th ed. 1950, 337–343.

[356] Cf. Deuteronomy, 5, 8 (Second Commandment). Cf. also the comparison of God's word with a falling star in M. Buber: Einsichten, 1953, 27.

[357] Looking back I also notice that I have not wielded the Occam's Razor as much as it could have been used. It seems that an inquiry into the fundamentals of justice of the same scope as the present one could be carried out by resorting to fewer *„entia"*, that is, to fewer principles and notions than were resorted to here. However, I am not sure whether this would promote the clarity

problem is the criteria of supreme goodness. Since I conceived the *Summum Bonum* as the value which occupies the apex in the hierarchy of values to which the just belongs, it is disquieting that the criteria relating to this paramount value were left open. The failure to point them out seems to leave our highest valuations at large, if not exposed to arbitrariness. This situation seems to reflect somehow adversely also on the axiotic status of the just, justness, and justice[358]. Is it possible to determine the criteria of the supreme goodness? Or is it possible to indicate the ways for finding them?

About the *Summum Bonum* I can say that it is the value to be experienced in boundless Care; it is an axiotic attribute to appear as the noëma of this noësis. Boundless Care, however, means for me a loving concern, a circumspect solicitude, a considerate affection, which concern, solicitude, and affection are all-encompassing[359]. It means the *ápeiron* of our surmisable emotions of ultimate love and anxiety which have come together in a unity. In this unity the wealth of human experience gathered by the mind in its movement away from boundless anxiety towards boundless love has not been lost but is retained in a lasting rule of *mnemosyne*. But speaking of the *Summum Bonum* as of a value *to be* experienced, not *being* experienced, is there a purpose in seeking its criteria at all? Are there criteria for the attribution of a value which is posited as unknowable? Are there criteria for the attribution of only a surmisable value? The answer to these questions seems to be „No". If a value has no actuality for us, the criteria of the corresponding valuations must also have no actuality for us. A noumenal value such as the *Summum Bonum* can have neither objective nor subjective criteria. This does not, however, entail that the attributions of this value cannot be but arbitrary. Valuations may rightly be reproached as arbitrary if subjective or objective criteria are available for them but are not resorted to. If they are not available, valuations are beyond the reproach of arbitrariness. Our proper attitude in this situation seems to lie in the *epoché* of academic skepsis. This attitude does not imply that the valuating subject should withhold judgments in the particular problems confronting him but that he should hold in suspension the judgments at which he arrives in the sense that he abstains from passing

---

of presentation in the present scholarly situation in view of the fact that little attention has been paid to the research of the fundamentals of justice. Occam's Razor can be successfully and extensively used only where there has already been a considerable rational penetration into a field of knowledge.

358 On the relations between the *Summum Bonum* and justice cf. W. Fuchs: Neoklassik in der Rechtsphilosophie, 1954, 1—60. Note especially this writer's critical remark that in Radbruch's doctrine of justice the *bonum* has been a great mystery, a *Noli me tangere,* almost something uncanny *(Unheimliches),* something numinous, p. 4.

359 With the notion of Care cf. the notion of *agape* as understood by P. Tillich: Love, Power, and Justice, 1954, 119. Cf. also Tillich's notion of creative justice, the functions of which are listening, giving, and forgiving, p. 84.

final judgments. That is, he should be constantly aware of the provisional character of his prizings involving the *Summum Bonum* and refrain from arrogating to any of them a dignity definitely superior to that of others claiming recognition.

Having come to the conclusion that criteria of supreme goodness are not available to finite understanding, I now apprehend that the peak of the hierarchy of values must appear to us enshrouded in a cloud. But even though we cannot see it, we cannot say that it does not exist. And even though we cannot hope to reach it, we still may strive towards it. The striving for the apprehension of the *Summum Bonum* seems to be itself a value of high axiotic dignity. This value, an axiotic circumstance, can be named Reason, which is a value of wayfaring, of *acheminement*. The axiotic attribute corresponding to Reason is the reasonable, and the criteria by reference to which the attribution of the latter is substantiated are the criteria of reasonableness. The noësis of the reasonable is a familiar experience; no less familiar than the experiences of the true, the just, and the beautiful. There are both subjective and objective criteria for the attribution of the reasonable. The first set of the objective criteria of reasonableness are to be found in the principles essential for sustaining and promoting life[360]. Life is a fundamental circumstance of human existence. Denying life, we assail all our axiotic strivings withal: these strivings presuppose living entities. But life does not appear to have a completely fixed value. Its worth depends on its correspondence to principles determining its forms and levels — principles which can be found in the tenets of high morality and of the world's great religions. These tenets appear to be the second important set of the objective criteria of reasonableness. There is a considerable, even though not always manifest, agreement between these tenets, but there is also a conflict. In any case the tenets of religion have significance for man only when they have passed through an interpretative process of the mind. For the conduct of this process there are settled principles existing in the accepted high standards of scholarship, the essentials of which are admirably worded in Francis Bacon's description of the scientific mind[361]. These standards constitute the third important set of the objective criteria of reasonableness. The observance of high standards of scholarship tempers moral and religious tenets with

[360] Cf. P. W. Kurtz: Human Nature, Homeostasis, and Value, 1956, 17, Philosophy and Phenomenological Research, 36, at 57.

[361] See Bacon: *De Interpretatione Naturae Proemium* in *Works*, ed. by J. Spedding et al., 1887, vol. III, p. 518 ff.: „*Me ipsum autem ad veritatis contemplationes, quam ad alia, magis fabrefactum deprehendi; ut qui mentem et ad rerum similitudem (quoad maximum est) agnoscendam satis mobilem, et ad differentiarum subtilitates observandas satis fixam et intentam haberem; qui et quaerundi desiderium, et dubitandi patientiam, et meditandi voluptatem, et asserendi cunctationem, et disponendi sollicitudinem tenerem; quique nec novitatem affectarem, nec antiquitatem admirarem, et omnem imposturam odissem*". For an analogous description of the „philosophic mind" see A. Boyce Gibson: Should Philosophers Be Kings? 1939, 9–13.

the principle of enlightened doubt[362]; in many cases it should show their compatibility and complementarity; in some cases it may bring to the full vision of *homo religiosus* their horrifying unacceptable implications. The principle of enlightened doubt does not import Pyrrhonic doubt. It is a principle of doubt free from any arrogance of exaggerated claims; it does not prevent me from smiling nor does it exclude me from a sentiment of devotion. Even being a doubter I can suffer to the extreme for the sake of my ideals still wondering why, and give my ultimate love to God, although I approach Him in doubt. In doubting I believe in God, since without doubt there is no object of belief but only of certain knowledge. Without doubt there is no faith and hope but certainty about what is and will be. And without doubt, I wonder whether there is even reasonable love and anxiety, that is, Care. Being a doubter I accept my ultimate obligations and set my ultimate hopes which would flow from the boundless Care I am capable of surmising, by way of a wager. But why should not this be by way of a wager? If God does not exist and if my transcendent hopes are impossibilities, I have nothing to loose but have a hope to win tranquility or even serenity in this life. If this world and the hereafter is run by a demon, then by striving for what I surmise to have the supreme goodness I may have the pleasure of defying this demon and the satisfaction of being engaged in a transcendent heroism, be it even but a heroism of Don Quixote.

The doubt operating in the „scientific mind" is not a doubt from which truth is expected to flow, but a doubt operating as a principle of discovery, keeping the mind constantly in search so that truth as *aletheia* would be in becoming for man[363] as a perpetual process of unconcealment of Being[364]. The subjective counterpart of this unconcealment is the sense of axiotic evidence which is relevant not only to the value „true" but to all fundamental values. Axiotic evidence may be conceived, however, as the ultimate criterion of validity only for the authentic Self. Since this Self appears to have no empirical existence but to be only a *limes* towards which the phenomenal Self can only perpetually approach, axiotic evidence is, in actuality, no absolutely trustworthy criterion of validity. It is a relatively trustworthy criterion where the valuating subject has respected all axiotic standards that would follow from Reason as realised in the historical situation to which he belongs.

I have quieted my mind about the criteria of the supreme goodness by satisfying myself that they are unavailable. I found comfort for

---

[362] Cf. P. Tillich: The Courage to Be, 2nd ed. 1953, 158: „Doubt dissolves the veil of Maya, it undermines the defense of mere opinions against ultimate reality."

[363] Cf. Gordon Allport's remarks on dogmatism made in his essay Becoming, 1955, 17 ff. Cf. also R. Polin: Against Wisdom, 1955, 16, Philosophy and Phenomenological Research, 1, at 11.

[364] Cf. L. Lavelle: Le Moi et Son Destin, 1936, 112 ff.; L. L. Fuller: American Legal Philosophy at Mid-Century, 1954, 6, Journal of Legal Education, 457, at 480.

their absence in the hope which lies in the criteria of reasonableness[365], culminating in the principle of radical but enlightened doubt[366]. I wonder what have I achieved towards answering the questions about the fundamentals of justice I posed in the First Discourse[367]. As far as I can judge my own inquiry, I may say that at least this has been done by me towards answering these questions: I have articulated the problem, which means, I have moved closer to the possibility of its clearer apprehension. If this judgment should be a self-deception, I trust I can say that I have at least made the realities of justice that confront us more problematic by pointing out problems which are not directly visible[368]. As the questions originally stood, they were only themes for a more extensive questioning. In the course of my study I attempted to clarify the references of the words by which these questions were asked, and to state a number of problems which these references seemed to raise. Thus I should have done something towards exposing the fundamentals of justice to the scrutiny of inquiring minds. Voicing a number of doubts which the elaboration of the themes of the fundamentals of justice raised for me, I hope I have indicated some pitfalls threatening inquiries into these themes. Whether and to what extent I have succeeded in avoiding these pitfalls myself, I am unable to see at present. I trust, however, that I have charted the ground somewhat for similar future inquiries, and even with my errors and oversights — provided that they are recognisable to other inquirers — have done something towards the apprehension of the fundamental principles of justice by challenging others to strive for more assured or assuring results.

Now at the end of my inquiry I feel the obligation to summarise its results in the form of answers to the questions with which I commenced the present essay. „Is there justice?“, I now can answer: „Yes, justice exists.“ „What is justice?“, I can answer: „Justice is a social situation to which the value ‚just‘ is attributed“ or „Justice is a social situation deemed to have justness“. „Can justice be known?“, I can answer: „Justice can be known.“ „How can justice be known?“, I can answer: „Justice can be known by apprehending the social situations to which the just is attributed and by apprehending the respective acts of attribution.“ „Ought justice to be done?“, I can answer: „Justice ought to be done as a rule, but not invariably.“ „When ought justice to be done?“, I can answer: „Justice ought to be done when the criteria of justness do not conflict with the criteria of validity by reference to which

365 On this doubt see George Santayana's delightful pages in his book Scepticism and Animal Faith, 4th impr. 1936, 1—41.

366 For this discussion of the criteria of reasonableness I have received essential stimulus from my friend Dr. Stevan Glichitch of the Faculty of Law of Sydney University.

367 These questions were: „Is there justice, and if there is, what is it?“, „Can justice be known, and if it can, how?“, „Ought justice to be done, and if it ought, when?“

368 Cf. Gustav Radbruch's view (Rechtsphilosophie, 4th ed. 1950, 173) that philosophy ought not to make life easy but problematic.

any other value of higher axiotic dignity than the *just is attributed.*" What these answers are exactly intended to convey can be seen, of course, only on the basis of essentially the whole of the foregoing study[369].

Here at the end of my inquiry I recall once more Kant's words: „If justice perishes, it is no longer of value for men to live on the earth." Do the conclusions at which I have arrived about justice in the present essay permit me to say that the value of man's life depends on justice in the sense of a concrete order, of a reality deemed to have justness? My immediate inclination is to answer this question by „No". If justice perishes but brotherly love, charity, and other social values of at least as high axiotic dignity as justice prevail, it should be still of value for men to live on the earth. But can such social situations become actualities without the actuality of justice? It seems to me that they cannot. Justice, even though defective, even though imperfectly achieved but still attempted, striven for under the norm of Reason, seems to me a basis required for the realisation of the ideas of felicity, morality, piety, and other axiotic standards of august content. Justice as an actuality appears to be a foundation-situation for man's social life and thereby also for his individual life[370]. It is not a part of the structure of the world but an entity that we ought constantly to try to bring into the world; it is an entity that ought to be a constant object of our Care[371]. Justice in the sense here in question is a concrete situation, an ontic entity, and as such it is subject to destruction „according to necessity and arrangement of time", to use the words of Anaximander. If justice perishes then, truly, it is of no value for men to live on the earth, because without it no other situations of worthwhile human existence would endure. And when justice has perished on the earth, the law of the Cosmos referred to by Anaximander concerning the destruction of „existing things"

[369] At the end of this inquiry I feel I should indicate what I apprehend the solution of the case to be the facts of which I stated at the beginning of my First Discourse.

On the basis of the foregoing study, the following can be said about this case: The eviction of the poor man was ostensibly just by reference to the criteria of justness objectivised in the norms of the positive law under which the eviction order was made. If it be assumed that the defendant attempted to found his opinion that he was unjustly treated on any axiotic principles at all, the decision was not just by reference to the defendant's subjective criteria of justness. Provided that the court's decision could not be based on the defendant's deserts (merits) properly so called but rather on mercy, pity, or charity that a public authority ought to have displayed, his proper complaint would have been that he was not charitably, or equitably (in the legal-philosophical sense) treated. If the judge had the power to give a charitable (an „equitable") relief to the defendant, his failure to do so seems to reflect, *prima facie*, adversely on his moral qualities. If he did not have such power, it could be expected that in considering the case he experienced Care, and made his decision reluctantly, with a heavy heart.

[370] Cf. Lord Justice Morris: The Spirit of Justice, 1954, 4.

[371] Cf. H. Fingarette: Psychoanalytic Perspective of Moral Guilt, 1955, 16, Philosophy and Phenomenological Research, 18, at 32.

may operate. This operation would entail that the earth itself as an „existing thing" might return to the *ápeiron* together with those entities which, having made the earth their scene, must by perishing expiate the injustice they have done. But is there a danger that justice will disappear altogether? It seems to me that this is almost inconceivable. As long as men inhabit the earth, at times injustice may utterly prevail over justice, but it surely cannot be absolutely victorious. The utter prevailing of injustice tends to render the craving for justice extreme[372]. In the folds of the actualities of injustice thus at least seeds of justice are preserved in the mode of potentiality as visions of justice. In times to come these seeds will find a chance to bring their hidden possibilities to life in a spring, summer, and autumn of justice from a winter which is, however, not the Cosmic Night.

These reflections raise the problems of the reality of justice; they call for a study of the processes in which justice is actualised, a study of its evolution and involution. They also invite inquiries into the results of these processes in history as well as in the present time. This study unavoidably leads to the problem of material justice, that is, to the problem of natural law as a body of decisive criteria of justness. But all these matters are specific themes of inquiry and as such beyond the scope of an essay as the present one was designed to be. I hope to be able to address myself to them in the course of my future work.

---

372 The craving for justice, the consciousness of a need for justice appears to be co-present with man's being in the world. Cf. A. E. Sutherland: The Law and One Man among Many, 1956, 94: „After all, man has survived — thus far — and surviving, is still conscious of a need for justice. The very presence of this aspiration, its continuance through all disappointment and doubt, should be a reason for our abiding wonder." The wonder to which Professor Sutherland refers is, as I understand, essentially also philosophical wonder; it is the wonder that poses philosophical problems of justice and calls for inquiries into the fundamentals of justice.

GPSR Compliance

The European Union's (EU) General Product Safety Regulation (GPSR) is a set of rules that requires consumer products to be safe and our obligations to ensure this.

If you have any concerns about our products, you can contact us on ProductSafety@springernature.com

In case Publisher is established outside the EU, the EU authorized representative is:

Springer Nature Customer Service Center GmbH
Europaplatz 3
69115 Heidelberg, Germany

Batch number: 10844655

Printed by Printforce, the Netherlands